Every morning, so far, I'm alive

A MEMOIR

Wendy Parkins

OTAGO

For M

Published by Otago University Press
Level 1, 398 Cumberland Street
Dunedin, New Zealand
university.press@otago.ac.nz
www.otago.ac.nz/press

First published 2019
Copyright © Wendy Parkins
The moral rights of the author have been asserted

ISBN 978-1-98-853161-8

Published with the assistance of Creative New Zealand

Editor: Caren Wilton
Design: Fiona Moffat
Front cover art copyright © Jane Puckey, 2018
Author photograph by Lori Satterthwaite

Printed in China through Asia Pacific Offset

Every

morning,

so far,

I'm alive

Contents

Isn't it plain the sheets of moss, except that
they have no tongues, could lecture
all day if they wanted about

spiritual patience? Isn't it clear
the black oaks along the path are standing
as though they were the most fragile of flowers?

Every morning I walk like this around
the pond, thinking: if the doors of my heart
ever close, I am as good as dead.

Every morning, so far, I'm alive. And now
the crows break off from the rest of the darkness
and burst up into the sky—as though

all night they had thought of what they would like
their lives to be, and imagined
their strong, thick wings.

MARY OLIVER, 'LANDSCAPE'

1.

Symptoms
are a
way of
thinking
about
difficult things

Please don't enter the waiting room more than five minutes before your scheduled appointment, the emailed instructions I had received a few days ago read. *The front door will be on the latch. Come in, lock it behind you, sit on the chair, and I will come and collect you at the appointed time.*

I wanted to be collected. To be gathered, disentangled, and put back together. At the appointed time.

So here I was, as instructed, sitting on an upright wooden chair in a white hallway. Next to the door, facing me, was a polished mahogany hall table, a pot of flawless white orchids centred exactly on top. The hallway was blocked off from the rest of the house by a folding white rice-paper screen but, looking up, I could see the upper floor through the stairwell. Everything was white: walls, ceilings, banister. It struck me that the house smelled of nothing. Everyone's house has its own unique aroma – musty or doggy, last night's curry or sickly-sweet air freshener – often only detectable by a visitor. This house revealed nothing of its life beyond the rice-paper screen.

Arriving early, I had initially waited outside in my car where I had been told to park. After a few minutes a woman had left the house, climbed into a blue hatchback and driven off down the street, only to stop after a few hundred metres. Was she unable to compose herself after a traumatic session? Or just checking her text messages before driving on?

The last time I had found myself in a waiting room like this I had (among other things) been mildly obsessed with suicidal women writers – Virginia Woolf, Sylvia Plath – but embarrassed by how clichéd such an obsession was. I even wrote a poem called 'Bottles of Milk by the Bed'.

After I reluctantly revealed to my then-psychiatrist my sense of hopelessness, he badgered me to confess how I was planning to opt out completely. *That is a very stupid idea*, he said. *You would be very stupid to try that. You would probably fail and end up a vegetable.* He was an angry man who often spent time in my sessions railing against the idiocies of the modern world, while I sat politely, waiting for my medication to kick in as he assured me it would, in another week or two. When I heard some years later that he had died of leukemia, I was ashamed to feel no compassion.

The time before that, the first time I had fallen apart – but what do I mean by falling apart? A 'nervous breakdown' is what it was called in Australia in the early 1970s, when it happened to my mother. That term sounds so dated and melodramatic now, as if evoking a still earlier time, like a black-and-white 1950s movie probably starring Susan Hayward (my mother's favourite actress). In the 1970s, lots of people's mothers seemed to have had nervous breakdowns, were prescribed Valium, went to hospital, were whispered about by the other mothers. But that's not the story I want to tell. This is not my mother's story.

And yet how best to describe what I first experienced in my final undergraduate year in the mid-1980s? Depression and agoraphobia, while technically correct diagnoses, lack the broad range of 'nervous breakdown', a term used since the early twentieth century to cover a multiplicity of symptoms involving both mind and body. Breakdown signals that life has been stopped in its tracks, normal existence interrupted. It implies inertia as well as disintegration. There is both a break – a rupture, a state of brokenness – and a downward trajectory towards what feels like a bottomless plunge into darkness, loss of meaning, loss of purpose, possibly never to surface again into the light. The 'nervous' part is rarely used any more, gone like the vials of smelling salts used by Victorian women succumbing to the vapours.

So, in the absence of a better alternative, breakdown will have to do.

During my first breakdown, then, when the normal fabric of life had been ruptured by a range of symptoms – frequent panic attacks, loss of appetite, loss of pleasure or interest in anything, hypersomnia, feeling worthless – I had received treatment from an understanding GP who helped far more than the benign psychiatrist to whom she referred me. He had said little and made no eye contact, although he occasionally wrote notes on my file while my mother waited outside his office. Mostly I retreated to books as therapy. Or as escape. I spent a long, idle year after graduation back at home with my parents, away from the city and all my friends. *Those miserable books you read*, my mother said, *no wonder you're unhappy*. Even Charlotte Brontë's *Shirley* she regarded with suspicion. But then I suppose I was a young woman languishing in the Australian equivalent of a country vicarage and fearing I was going mad. I bought a dog.

Thirty years later and now on the verge of my third breakdown, I was hoping that a bracing course of psychoanalytic therapy could prevent any further decline and reconcile me to life in England where I felt myself drifting, unmoored, about to founder entirely. If I were to map my mental health, a kind of geography of previous founderings, it would show two red flags marking the extremities of the Australian continent, from east to west: one in Sydney, the site of my first breakdown, the second in Perth a decade later. And then an amber flag on the South Island of New Zealand, where I had found relatively safe harbour in Dunedin for eight years after leaving Perth, managing to keep my propensity for depression and phobias within workable limits apart from occasional flare-ups, not-quite-crack-ups, before choosing to uproot again to southeast England. And now sitting in a Dover waiting room, as close to the edge as it was possible to be.

ᴥ

When the therapist opened the white door to her white room, she was wearing flowing linen trousers and a long loose blouse, an ensemble of white and beige, with a simple necklace of large wooden beads and her short blonde hair falling in natural curls. I sat opposite her in a room of pale Scandinavian furniture and textiles, feeling like the epitome of frumpiness.

With the exception of the two psychiatrists – the first ineffectual, the second angry – other therapists I had consulted over the years had been comforting and reassuring. My last therapist sometimes cried during my sessions when I described childhood episodes of what felt normal to me, a reaction I found both unnerving and deeply touching. This woman, however, gave nothing away. She regarded me attentively as I began to talk about why I was there but she didn't smile, or even nod. *You want to regain some joy in your life*, she summarised, after my account had petered out. I agreed, keeping to myself that *joy* is a word I have always disliked. It is my middle name.

She was my first therapist since moving to England from New Zealand two years previously, and at first I wondered if this was a cultural thing, whether English therapists were just more reticent, less informal than those I had met before. I felt diminished and exposed by the blankness with which she regarded me. A few sessions later I finally summoned the courage to tell her how intimidating I found her calm silence, the utter stillness with which she listened to me without offering any positive affect in response. *I am simply reflecting back what you convey*, she replied. Chilled and confused in equal measure, I left the white room, the white house, and never returned.

My need to escape from the white house and the woman whose apparent attention to me lacked any warmth stayed with me. When I arrived home that day I felt compelled to write it all down, like a purging, an expunging of something that had felt close to annihilation. Writing like that was not something I normally did even though, as a professor of English literature, writing was central to my working life. But writing about what hurt and scared me, what exposed me, was something I had avoided for a long time. After that day, I didn't write again for a long time.

That was in the spring.

In the summer, one stifling Sunday in July, I found myself in the carpark of the Eurotunnel terminal in Calais among hundreds of holidaymakers who were sitting on the grass, or walking their dogs, or chasing their children. All the trains were delayed. I walked in circles around the car park, beside myself with fear and anxiety, unable to return to my own car to wait with my husband and son for the final part of our long journey back from a holiday in the south of France. I had had a bad experience in the women's toilets – having to use a filthy, horribly stained cubicle – and now I wanted to pull off my own skin. Nowhere was safe, there was no exit from my constantly looping thoughts of doom.

Dogs, children, sunshine. People carrying cases of wine to their BMWs, eating burgers, licking ice cream.

I could think only of the possible contamination to which I had been exposed in the cubicle and which I was now powerless to expunge. The (bile-coloured?) stains clinging to the rim of the toilet bowl, unnoticed until I had locked the cubicle door and thus already entered – and touched – a space that could carry contagion, infection, disease.

By the time our train was due for departure I was exhausted, all my attention focused on the hand that had touched the toilet door, the flush button, repulsed and frightened of it in equal parts. It was part of me and there was nothing I could do about it. I had, of course, repeatedly rubbed sanitiser over my hands until they were grainy with it, unable to absorb any more gel, but I had no confidence that I was safe. I had wept at first, too, ashamed that my son and husband were seeing me in this state (again), but then I just shut down, sitting still and silent in the front seat of our car as we passed under the English Channel. The loud clattering of the metal train carriage containing our car was unable to drown out my inner monologue about impending catastrophe. When we arrived home, a short drive from the Eurotunnel port at Folkestone, I took an extra-long shower, unpacked, and then cooked a simple dinner for my family. The next day I returned to work, made small-talk, smiled, performed tasks like a normal person, like a person who isn't wishing someone would say, *You are unwell. You can't do this on your own. Let me help you.*

In the autumn that same year I received an invitation to speak at a symposium in my favourite region of Italy, all expenses paid. It was not only professionally gratifying, an exciting opportunity to develop a project close to my heart with an international network of scholars, but also promised a pleasant day or two of piazza-strolling and dining al fresco.

On the morning of my departure for the symposium I stopped to have a coffee with my husband on my way to the airport. As we stood at the counter waiting to be served, I heard the young barista say to his supervisor, *Send me home. I shouldn't be here.* He was laughing as he said this and his supervisor seemed not to take him seriously, but was he in fact unwell? Did he have something contagious? Would my coffee be safe to drink? Could I then embark on an international trip alone, knowing that I could be incubating some nasty bug that could strike me down in transit, in public, in an unfamiliar place?

At that moment I knew I would not be attending the symposium. I would take my suitcase home again and unpack all the clothes that I had neatly folded that morning. I would explain it somehow to my mystified husband. I would send my apologies to the symposium organisers. I would feel like a pathetic failure.

And all the time I would be worrying that I would become ill at some point over the next few days. Because I had drunk the coffee.

I didn't fall ill, but I felt like I had reached the nadir of my descent into contamination phobia and its associated OCD. Such episodes were all too familiar to me but this seemed a new low. For years I had managed to live by the feel-the-fear-and-do-it-anyway principle; now I seemed to have finally run out of the energy needed to maintain the façade of a functioning professional. Psychoanalyst Adam Phillips says it is as if a phobic person has their own private language, *a secretive exemption from shared meanings*, however absurd this may seem to other people. My phobia was not a private language in which I wanted to be fluent. I wanted to inhabit a world shared with other people, people who could travel, shake hands or use public toilets without terror. I *knew* how absurd my reaction was. The isolation and the shame of suffering from contamination phobia, the inability to admit – even to my husband – that because of an overheard remark in a café I was crippled by fear, with a racing heart and shaking hands, forced to abandon my trip and retreat home to (comparative) safety, only added to my misery.

As a phobic person, then, I led a kind of double life, necessarily concealing my phobia from others – my family and friends, my colleagues and students – hoping that the screaming terror in my head was audible only to me. Of course I didn't tell the symposium organisers I suffered from contamination phobia and OCD, merely that I had taken ill.

At the same time I knew that I was also concealing things from myself, even if I didn't quite know what those things were. *In the phobic fantasy*, Phillips writes,

> you convince a part of yourself that the bad things are elsewhere only because there is really no elsewhere (or the only real elsewhere is the place you cannot put parts of yourself) … but if one can tolerate some of one's 'badness' – meaning recognize it as yours – then one can take some fear out of the world.

Symptoms, then, *are a way of thinking about difficult things.* A phobia sets in place (or tries to set in place) a clear distinction between what is acceptable and what is dangerous. As disabling as a phobia is, it also offers the phobic person the fantasy that the bad things she fears can be held elsewhere, outside, away from her; that what is unbearable can be kept apart from the self, and therefore that the self can be tolerated. In my world, the bad things were all around me, making the most ordinary stuff seem life-threatening, like those Hollywood movies where deadly plagues are quickly spread through innocuous, everyday things like a bowl of peanuts in a bar or a shared bus ride. That was just everyday life for me. Finding a way to take some of the fear out of the world seemed futile. The world *was* scary. Germs *do* lurk everywhere (especially in bowls of peanuts in bars). But I knew that I was bad, too. I could never be sure I wasn't carrying germs or viruses. The bad stuff was outside but also inside. There was no escape, no way to inhabit the 'elsewhere' where I could tolerate my own 'badness', where it was okay to be less than perfect.

2.

Ever vigilant

Here are some dreadful things:

> Shaking hands
> Sitting next to a pale or drawn stranger
> Door handles
> Taxis
> Aeroplane seat-belts
> Supermarket checkout operators (especially pale or drawn ones)
> A stranger's pen
> Library books
> Students' essays
> Pharmacies, doctor's surgeries, hospitals
> Public computer terminals
> Poles in the Tube (the safety features, not people from Eastern Europe)
> Hotel rooms

Petrol stations
Elevator buttons
EFTPOS terminals
Tradespeople in my house
Babies or small children
Self-serve cafeterias and salad bars
The 'vom_t' word
Did I mention public toilets?

These things filled me with dread. At least one of them (usually more) terrified me on a daily basis. They were *dangerous, perilous*, which the *Oxford English Dictionary* may consider an obsolete meaning of 'dreadful' but always seemed particularly apt to me: these bad things imperilled me. They *excited fear or aversion* (as the *OED* continues) and, as a result, I was always on watch, in a heightened state of awareness, unable to let my guard down for a moment. My daughter, M, joked that my personal motto was *ever vigilant*.

Not only does a phobia terrify and render the sufferer helpless, it also makes the ordinary seem unusually charged, so that I am simultaneously fixated with and estranged from the mundane stuff all around me. In the early decades of the twentieth century, modernist writers were hailed as revolutionary for creating a sense of estrangement from the banalities of modern life in their novels and poems. Phobics are not revolutionaries, they are just scared and exhausted by the constant assault of overly charged objects and experiences. Nothing can be taken for granted; everything resonates with the potential for catastrophic significance. *To be terrified by a pigeon*, Adam Phillips observes in his essay on phobias, *is a way of making it new, a kind of quotidian sublime*. I didn't want the dreadful things to be new or exciting, I wanted them to be comfortingly familiar. I didn't want to be swept away by the sublime when I was just trying to make it through the day.

Phobics would welcome more banality in their lives.

I would like to hope that most people don't regard a petrol pump or a stranger's pen as powerful objects, radiating danger and terror like an electrical charge. I would like to think that for many (most?) people such objects are simply tools of daily life, a means of carrying out vital but rudimentary tasks. These objects don't draw undue attention to themselves, they are almost invisible, so that normal people can just get on with the important stuff that these tools make possible.

I would like to hope that others are not, like me, stuck at the point where the ordinary becomes un-doable, or where the effort involved in the ordinary precludes enjoyment or concentration on what is meant to be the main focus, some important task or event. Because that pen, that handshake, that petrol pump, looms large in my mind like an evil talisman, long after it has passed from my sight or vicinity.

I would like to think that other people have the kind of mind-space available – to think, to dream, to imagine, to communicate, to enjoy – that is possible when one does not need to be ever vigilant against all the bad things that wait for a moment's distraction in order to spoil, to ruin, to infect or contaminate you. For me, daily life involved a complex and demanding set of survival techniques.

I always carried my own pen.

I practised balancing, legs braced and slightly apart, on crowded trains so that I wouldn't need to hold on to any support.

I used self-service lanes at supermarkets and was weak with gratitude when 'contactless' payment became a thing.

I pushed doors open with my foot.

I survived on my own snacks or just skipped lunch at conferences or work events to avoid communal utensils or food platters.

I avoided social situations where there would be babies or small children.

Needless to say, hand sanitiser was my constant companion, and my parting comment whenever a family member left the house was always, *Do you have hand sanitiser with you?*

I am ashamed to say that I have feigned tendonitis in my wrist (long after it had healed) to avoid shaking hands.

I have asked flight attendants to move me to a different seat because *I suffer from claustrophobia* (somehow less humiliating to confess than contamination phobia sparked by the passenger sitting next to me).

I happily walk across a city if it means avoiding public transport or a taxi. Avoidance, in fact, is the most common strategy. Research is a vital part of my profession as an academic, but libraries are full of books touched by other people, and visiting the British Library requires a train trip to London. London is dreadful. Too many people, too many germs.

Even seeking treatment for my condition required exposure to the dreadful. One of the reasons I doggedly resisted trying medication to alleviate my symptoms for so long was that I knew that, in order to get a prescription, I would have to visit the doctor's surgery and the pharmacy which, by definition, rank highly as possible sites of contamination.

Before fear of contamination became my phobia *du jour*, I succumbed to bouts of crippling agoraphobia which first began to surface in my mid-teens in Sydney. I started to have panic attacks just walking to the bus stop on school days. Home felt like the only safe space in a widening world that could look enticing but which I feared was mostly hostile. There were many days when I turned back and walked home again from the bus stop, changed into my pyjamas and crawled into bed. I didn't know I was experiencing panic attacks; it just felt like crippling nausea, trembling and dizziness. Everything was too bright and too close and too loud and I couldn't breathe properly. But it all felt better when I lay in bed and pulled up the covers. As a small child, I was often poorly, spending weeks in bed with bronchitis, ear infections, tonsillitis, so there was something comfortingly familiar in a retreat to my bed. My parents were concerned, trying to tempt my failing appetite with the kind of sweet treats I usually enjoyed, taking me regularly to the doctor or for the tests he recommended, but they mostly let me be.

When my agoraphobia started, my family had recently returned to Sydney after seven years in a small town on the north coast of New South Wales. Irish writer Elizabeth Bowen called her memoir of childhood *Seven Winters*, referring to a formative period in her early life, distinctive as much for the fact that it was divided between two homes – one in Dublin and the other a grander ancestral home at Bowen's Court in County Cork – as for the lingering influence on her later life of what she called the *semi-mystical topography of childhood*. For me, *Seven Summers* would be a more apt title: my first seven years of life were spent in Sydney; the next seven in a small town by the beach, surrounded by bush, where in my memory it is always summer. Then back to Sydney, where I remained – apart from a few short absences – until I was almost 30. (And then Perth, and then Dunedin, and then England.) Moving house has been so common for me that it is often difficult to tell whether home is somewhere I want to return to or somewhere I want to escape from.

My teenage agoraphobia gradually dissipated over the course of a year, without treatment and without formal diagnosis, as I adjusted to life in a new place. Only when it returned with a vengeance when I was 20, accompanied by depression, was I able to recognise what I had experienced at 15, when I had missed a lot of school with mystery stomach illnesses, had a series of diagnostic tests that all came back negative, lost considerable weight, gave up sport. But, at its worst in my early 20s and then again 10 years later when I was a fledgling academic, my agoraphobia was so severe that I couldn't leave my room, never mind the house. Shallow, accelerated breathing would give me palpitations and I would start to shake. I would think that I was either going to throw up or pass out – or both. I never did but that made absolutely no difference to the overwhelming fear that I would be rendered helpless in a public place: out of control and vulnerable. Leaving the safety of home felt life-threatening and required the kind of courage that would leave me drained of energy. I have heard agoraphobia described as the fear of panic attacks – the fear of fear – and this makes sense to me: the triggers for the fear can vary and multiply. What remains constant is the sense of terror and its bodily impact, and therefore the need to avoid that terror at all costs.

Apart from that first bout of agoraphobia at 15, my subsequent episodes of phobia have typically been a by-product of depression. Whenever I start to slide into depression – a condition that snakes its way through all the branches of my family tree – I suffer a flare-up of some form of phobia, because depression robs me of the energy required to remain on guard in a world of potential dangers. In the perfect circle of neurosis, the phobia then also exacerbates the depression; life becomes more circumscribed by avoidance and fear until it hardly seems worth the effort to get up in the mornings. At times like these, navigating everyday activities pushes me to my limits of endurance.

Over the years, when agoraphobia surfaced, I tried a range
of treatment — medication, counselling, psychotherapy, cognitive
behavioural therapy — culminating in a two-week intensive course at
a clinic in Perth that finally seemed to work. My agoraphobia receded
and I regained the world: I was able to leave the house without fear.
I could deliver lectures; eat in restaurants; go to the cinema; travel. I
could begin sentences with *When I used to have agoraphobia* and not
feel that I was tempting fate by even naming my tormentor.

Somehow, though, after I had been symptom-free for years, the
thought patterns that had first triggered agoraphobia began to morph
into something much more insidious, a fear that could engulf me
even within my own home, not just out in the wider world. The
microscopic form of my fears now — bacteria, viruses, germs — in no
way lessened their danger or my terror that they would overwhelm
me. Safety eluded me; even my own skin could contaminate me if
I touched an infected surface. The breath that I drew into my body
could be the source of some sickening contagion that could fester
deep inside me. After I had moved to New Zealand for a career
promotion (with my husband and two children, then aged four and
14), I experienced occasional downward spirals into depression,
contamination phobia and/or OCD but never hit rock bottom, that
state of brokenness where normal life becomes impossible. I soldiered
on.

During one episode of decline, however, I braced myself to
tackle the ordeal of the weekly supermarket shopping on a Saturday
morning. Pushing my shopping trolley, I entered the first aisle (with
my sleeves pulled down over my hands to avoid direct contact with
the trolley handle, of course) and saw an abandoned trolley, piled
high with shopping, while two supermarket workers were busy with
mops, buckets and spray cleaners beside it. My heart began to pound,
my mouth was bone dry, my hands were shaking. I knew what had
happened. I had no doubt that I could decode the signs and instantly
arrive at their meaning. A parent had been shopping with a small child
who had v___ted in the supermarket aisle, requiring parent and child
to flee with their shopping incomplete, and leaving the staff to clean

up the mess. To this day I have no idea what happened in that aisle. But I immediately backed away, abandoned my own empty trolley, and left the supermarket, even trying not to breathe lest there were airborne contaminants lingering.

I drove the short distance home and attempted to compose myself, relieved that no one else was there to witness my distress. My husband was watching our son's football match; our now-adult daughter had recently moved out to her own place. After 10 minutes or so, realising that my family would return in an hour and wonder why there was no food for lunch, I decided to visit a different supermarket, even though that raised my anxiety further because my phobia made me a creature of habit and I didn't like going to unfamiliar places. Nevertheless, I left the house again, still a little shaky and obsessing over the potential exposure to contamination I had just suffered, and promptly realised I had locked my car keys, house keys and phone inside. Now what? I was terrified, ashamed of my own stupidity and cowardice, and at my wits' end. It was midwinter in Dunedin.

What happened next was something that, even at the time, in my distressed state, I wondered if I would one day look back on as an amusing anecdote (*Remember that time?*). It involved dragging our longest ladder from the shed and positioning it precariously below the only open window – the bathroom window, slightly ajar, and *possibly* large enough for me to squeeze through. Once I had made it up the ladder to the window ledge, which I could just reach by standing on tiptoe, I realised that the only way in was head first, given my wobbly position on the ladder and the angle of the window opening. So I pushed on and in till my hands were clutching the sink (directly below the window in the bathroom) and my legs were waving in the air, free of any contact with the ladder. I could not possibly go back, as the ladder was now out of reach of my toes, but how could I fold my body to avoid crashing head first to the tiled bathroom floor? I pictured my husband and son coming home to find me unconscious with a bleeding head injury, sprawled on the floor.

I don't know how long I balanced there, neither in nor out, wondering how the hell my life had come to this point. How stupid to be afraid of shopping trolleys and door handles and small children and all the other ordinary stuff of daily life! How could I call myself an intelligent person if I couldn't perform basic tasks? What if my colleagues knew how stupid I was? What if my students knew that I was a quivering wreck much of the time?

There was only so long I could balance in such a ridiculous, not to mention uncomfortable, position. Eventually I committed fully to entering, awkwardly manoeuvring sideways until I could place my weight on the small cabinet next to the sink. I then dragged my legs in so that I landed in the sink before rolling onto the floor, avoiding heavy impact by some miracle rather than any natural flexibility on my part.

Five minutes later I left the house again – with my keys this time – and faced the strange supermarket before returning home, drained and ashamed. Definitely not my finest hour.

Much of the time, in fact, I felt as stupid and humiliated by my disorder as I did when I was dangling from my bathroom window. How could I not just 'think' myself out of it? And yet, at the same time, because I needed to be always alert and aware of what anyone around me was doing or saying, I had to be as smart and switched on as possible. I was always on patrol; I could never be clever enough to outwit my enemies – germs, bacteria, viruses – but had to marshal all my resources anyway. I couldn't trust anyone else to pay attention closely enough to know where the dangers were.

Who has touched what?

Who looks as if they might be contaminated with something I could catch?

How can I inhabit this space, perform this task, maintain an appearance of normality, rather than dissolving into total panic?

Can I eat this food that someone else has prepared for me?

Can *I* prepare food that I can eat?

Will I poison my family, or my dinner guests, through letting my guard down or my attention wander for one fatal moment while cooking? Best not to risk it. Ever vigilant. When in doubt, avoid, discard, destroy.

My family has on more than one occasion had to deal with the fact that the planned dinner I had started to cook needed to be disposed of due to the meat looking or smelling funny, the vegetables feeling questionable, or the jar or tin not opening in a way that I could be sure meant it had been properly sealed. *A late change of plan, kids – it's vegetarian pasta again!* I stand in the kitchen with a racing heart and shaking hands, weeping, washing my hands repeatedly but never feeling certain that everything is safe. Have I inadvertently cross-contaminated ingredients? What have I touched? What needs to be cleaned? What if my hands can never be properly clean?

To avoid this kind of situation, I self-medicated with glasses of chardonnay while cooking. It damped down the worst of the panic and anxiety and meant that (most of the time) an edible meal ended up on the table. My long-suffering husband learned that it was a waste of time to try to reason with me about food safety and no longer tried to stop me throwing out food that didn't meet my phobic standards, or that he knew I would not be able to eat.

❦

This time, in England and in my early 50s, soon after I had walked out on the Scandi-blanc therapist, I watched an episode of *Obsessive Compulsive Cleaners*, a programme I had until then assiduously avoided lest it give me ideas about previously unknown sources of germs or contamination that would restrict my daily life even further. When I didn't think I could feel any more afraid, I thought, *what the hell? Why not be (virtually) among my people for an hour?*

After my initial reaction to the OCD sufferers (*wow, she cleans her toilet 15 times A DAY?*), I was surprised to find that the premise I had assumed was exploitative (set up a clash between two different kinds of crazies – OCD sufferers and hoarders – thus allowing smugly normal viewers to enjoy the ensuing freak-show) resulted instead in a kind of discovery of compassion and empathy between the participants. The OCD sufferers and the hoarders each encountered the radical other whom they initially considered utterly bizarre. They had no common ground and regarded each other with horror, amusement or superiority. Instead of the freak show I had expected, however, it became a lesson in everyday ethics, how to live in a world with people who are nothing like you, whose love-objects and hate-objects are opposite to your own. So far, so good.

But – and here's the thing – it seemed to me that the final lesson of the programme was also about the *benefits* of OCD: having homes and public spaces that were clean and hygienic was a social good.

An obsession with expunging filth was kind of therapeutic after all. *Bleach is our friend,* as one OCD sufferer said. And while all the OCD cleaners reported positive outcomes through this form of extreme de-sensitisation therapy, from which they derived a sense of personal achievement, not only was there no simplistic suggestion that they could be fully cured by the experience they had undergone in a single episode, but rather there was a kind of acceptance of their condition.

I was humbled by watching it. It was not just that their homes were immeasurably cleaner than mine; I envied the new sense of calm they seemed to have attained through self-acceptance. I know this is the kind of happy ending these programmes require, but I had never before entertained the possibility of making peace with my phobic obsessions and the ensuing compulsive behaviour. I saw my illness as an unspeakable affliction that shamed me and would always blight my existence. How could I possibly learn to live with my vulnerability to dirt and danger?

3.

Bloom where you are planted

Aside from regular self-medication with chardonnay, my other reliable coping mechanism was a daily walk with the dog. Down the village high street, up a side road past the allotments, along a hedge-lined lane through apple and pear orchards leading to the bluebell wood. Rain or shine, summer or winter. The dog seemed to like it too.

Random snippets of poetry would often run through my head on these walks. *Open unto the fields, and to the sky. Murmuring of innumerable bees. Season of mists and mellow fruitfulness.* One Wordsworthian phrase – *hedge-rows, hardly hedge-rows* – almost became a mantra while walking, which may say as much about my limited knowledge of English poetry (I've always preferred novels) as it does about my obsessive thought patterns.

My daily dog-walks through the Kentish countryside were, then, mediated by an aesthetic distance, as if I was inhabiting a poem or a painting rather than being immersed in a real place. Having grown

up on the other side of the world, much of what I saw around me
now – trees, birds, flowers – I initially only recognised from literature
or art, like the time I heard the first cuckoo of spring, my first cuckoo
ever, and knew instantly what it was. It was not that these walks
were not calming, or that the landscape wasn't beautiful, but I didn't
feel it in the same way as I responded to the antipodean bush or the
beach. In childhood, I hadn't experienced nature through the prism
of a literature of place because I was exposed to very little Australian
literature at school. (Henry Kendall's 'Bellbirds' was apparently
the only Australian nature poem, according to my primary-school
education.) I may have cried when Judy was killed by a falling branch
but *Seven Little Australians* didn't consciously shape my relationship
with nature. Instead, most of the books I read immersed me in a
relentlessly British landscape, a place of oak trees and hawthorn and
foxgloves and snow, things that were all as unknown to me as the
idiom in which the children spoke to each other (*Don't be so beastly,
Edmund!*).

Growing up in Australia – *a place with more geography than
architecture*, as Tim Winton puts it – I played in the bush, often
barefoot. I particularly liked to build huts or dens: arranging fallen
branches as a shelter, bending and shaping long tufty grasses to make
places to sit or lie, sweeping clear the dirt floor with a twig broken
from a gum tree, decorating the space with interesting rocks or
flowering weeds that wilted almost instantly in the heat.

The children of the neighbourhood would set off on walks
through the bush behind my house – there were no paths, we just
made our way through the less dense spaces in the undergrowth
towards a creek we knew was there somewhere. Some days we found
it. We often walked around in circles, lost our sense of direction, spent
hours in the bush, but, somehow, these were things I was allowed to
do. There were occasional snakes, of course, so we carried sticks and
stepped carefully over any fallen logs in our path. Ticks were also a
regular nuisance (and needed to be painfully extracted with tweezers
or doused with methylated spirits to force them to back out of their
new fleshy home). I seemed particularly prone to have ticks on my
head, and my mother would find them when she was plaiting my hair
for school or – on one memorable occasion – when she had spent

27

ages curling my hair in rags before a friend's birthday party. When the tweezers initially failed to extract the tick, copious amounts of 'metho' were applied, with the result that I eventually went late to the party with a large patch of damp, dead-straight hair among the ringlets and smelling like a paint shop.

I know my mother was anxious about my safety during these bush rambles but she rarely forbade them. Or perhaps never forbade them effectively enough. She may not have known quite how far we roamed or what we were poking with sticks. I was usually an obedient child, but I was less compliant when it came to outdoor play after we moved to a small coastal town when I was seven. For instance, although my mother insisted I wear shoes to school – an entirely normal practice in the city but seemingly optional at my country primary – each day after I passed out of sight from our house I would take off my sandals and place them in my schoolbag. I would only put them on my dirty feet again when I reached the same point on my way home in the afternoon. I didn't know that one reason so many children went shoeless to school in the warmer months was because their families could not afford footwear all year round. I just wanted to blend in and seem like a country kid, rather than the city girl who was teased for the way she talked.

Up until then, as a small child in the suburbs, I had manifested an early aversion to dirt. In my mother's telling, I would apparently run back into the house to have my hands washed every time they became dirty or sticky, and it is true that in photographs of those years taken in the back garden I am usually wearing a pinafore-apron over my neat clothes. She paints a picture of me as a fastidious child who was innately repulsed by dirt, but pinafores don't magically appear at the whim of a child, do they? I don't recall other children my age wearing them. In photographs I look more like a child from the 1940s or 50s – pudding-bowl haircut, pinafore over a smocked dress, home-knitted cardigans – than the mid-1960s.

I am similarly puzzled by another memory from the pinafore period. On washing day my mother would spend long periods of time labouring over the old-fashioned washing machine (with a hand-wringer on top) in the outdoor laundry (it does sound like the 1940s, doesn't it?). She was – understandably – usually in a bad mood on such days and I would play in the garden or sit on the back steps next to the laundry while she worked. My mother was always an assiduous and loyal consumer of cleaning products and I remember that her bleach of choice came in a green and white striped metal bottle with a red plastic lid. For some reason, I was fascinated by these bottles, and would ask if I could play with them after they were empty. She would hand the bottle to me, with a strict injunction not to open the lid or try to swallow any dregs.

But I always would.

It was disgusting; the toxic smell took my breath away and the searing sensation of swallowing even a few drops made me choke and splutter. My mother would yell at me.

The next week on washing day I would ask again and she would give me the green and white bottle, issue the same warning. There would be just a few drops left. I would unscrew the lid and swallow them. I would splutter and shudder. She would yell.

I can't recall now (although my guess is that it is probably significant) what came first: the prohibition or the ingestion? Did the prohibition incite my disobedience, planting an idea that would not otherwise have occurred to me? Or did a childish experiment, triggered by the allure of the fascinating bottle, with its shiny red plastic lid perfect for a small hand to twist, lead to a prohibition intended to prevent it happening again?

Why neither of us learned from this experience but seemed doomed to repeat it remains a mystery. Did I want to be clean on the inside too? Or did the acrid burning taste give me a visceral understanding of what transgression felt like? Was I challenging maternal authority? Or trying to get her attention?

In my mother's place, I think I would have assumed that a smart and generally pliable child would learn from the unpleasant experience and not repeat it. And I can imagine the whiny eagerness with which I begged for the bottle, assuring her I only wanted to play with it – it was smooth to hold and it rolled well along the sloping pathway, making a tinkling, tinny sound – and so, each week, she was persuaded and gave it to me. Now, though, I can't help thinking, *why did she keep giving me the friggin' bottles?*

My father regularly told me stories about his idyllic childhood in a small town on a river not far from where we lived after we left Sydney, mostly involving climbing trees to raid birds' nests for eggs (but always ensuring one egg was left untouched). He taught me to observe and identify many native birds – from their flight or their song as much as by their plumage – so that today I still instinctively scan for birds in any new environment.

Even more than birds and the bush, though, I loved the beach as a child. Like most Australians of my generation, my childhood can be tracked through family photographs taken at the beach or some similar body of water: a river, a rock pool, or just an inflatable kiddy pool in the garden. As a toddler in such photographs, I start to sport what apparently was always known as my fishing hat. The hat itself changed over the years from its earliest manifestation as a fetching yellow straw hat with a black grosgrain hatband, perched on my bowl-cut bob. A later fishing hat I recall was a pink straw 'coolie' style, decorated with raffia flowers, prickly and enchanting in equal parts. Whatever its form, however, a fishing hat was *de rigueur* on long hot days spent at a quiet spot on the river called the Crossing, in the small town where my father grew up and where we had often spent summer holidays before the move from Sydney. I would paddle in the warm shallows, the river sand soft and silky under my feet, watching tiny silver fish skim improbably in an inch or two of water. Eventually, I would doze in the shade of the she-oaks on the river bank, lulled by the heat and the distinctive whooshing sound of the breeze in the branches, while the adults – my parents and an uncle and aunt or two – stood, ankle-deep in the river, casting lines into the deeper water until dusk.

Between the ages of seven and 14, being close to water became part of daily life. I went to sleep at night listening to the waves and most days, in my memory at least, my family went down to the beach – often just to stroll – after school, on hot summer evenings or wintry weekends. My father, a collector of shells as well as a watcher of birds, taught me to look out for the cowrie shells that often washed up on our favourite stretch of sand (the small tiger cowries were the most prized). In summer, spoilt for choice, we would vary our swimming destinations. We could go to the main surfing beach, or to the shelly beach via a dirt road that wound through bush at the bottom of our

street. If the surf was rough or it was too windy, we could drive a
few minutes to a swimming spot on the river, sheltered by a nearby
island, where the water was always calm and warmer than the ocean
(although often crowded for that reason). If the tides were right,
we could drive a little north of our town to another beach where a
narrow tidal channel coursed its way through the sand to the breakers
in curving loops, creating a swift flow of water that was ideal for
floating down, either on your back or on something inflatable, if you
remembered to bring it.

One Boxing Day when I was about 10, we had gone to this beach
and conditions were perfect: you could float on your back at what felt
like an exhilarating speed through the curves of the channel, down to
the shallows at the edge of the waves, then stand and run back up the
side of the sandy channel and do it all over again. As the rushing water
carved away at the banks, the sand kept collapsing into the water –
often aided by my feet, for the pleasure of watching the chunks of
wet sand break loose like icebergs, crash into the water and dissolve,
sometimes taking me with them so that I plunged unexpectedly into
the waist-deep water. Between the floating and the sand-crashing,
time flew by until you suddenly realised you were completely
exhausted and ravenous.

And that your new bluebird signet ring, a Christmas present from
the day before, was no longer on your finger. *That'll be halfway to New
Zealand by now*, my father yelled. As much as I mourned the ring's
loss and felt guilty about my negligent custodianship, I was fascinated
by the image of the vast expanse of ocean that had swallowed it up,
and it was comforting to imagine my ring washing up on a beach
on the other side of the Tasman Sea in a few days' time. (I took my
father's hyperbole as fact.) Looking back, that was the first time that I
entertained the idea of New Zealand as a place of refuge, a destination
where lost things might be found.

The beach shaped our weather – bringing strong sea breezes on
hot summer afternoons, or storms with torrential rain in autumn – as
well as the culture of the small town. For teenagers, the only place to
gather was the beach. The boys surfed, the girls watched and made
occasional forays into the waves to cool off from endless sunbathing,
careful to ensure that our 1970s string bikinis survived the onslaught

of the surf intact. (It was sometimes a losing – and mortifying – battle.) We all learned to smoke hiding out in the sand dunes. As a relentlessly good girl (smoking was my only, and very occasional, vice), I soon realised that the beach crowd was never going to accept me and, more than that, I didn't want to be a part of it. For a time in my teens, then, I lost my love of the beach, associating it with social exclusion and small-town confinement.

Long after my adolescent peers had opted out of family activities, though, I still went beachcombing (out of sight from the surfing clique) or on Sunday drives with my family. We were never campers or intrepid hikers, and much of my experience of the landscape was gained looking through a car window from the back seat. Every track turning off the sealed road we were driving along fascinated me. I would imagine walking down it alone, picturing the hypothetical destination. Sometimes my father would risk turning down one of these precarious dirt roads and we might arrive at an unexpected view over a valley spread before us, or be immersed in a cool green rainforest glade where the only sounds were the running of an unseen stream and the distinctive call of whipbirds. More commonly, such dirt roads came to a dead end at a locked farm gate, or petered out into sand, threatening to bog down the wheels of the family sedan and leave us stranded. Miraculously, we never were. We took our beautiful surroundings – and our safe place in it – for granted. We drove, we looked, maybe took a walk, then came home again for tea.

To my Evangelical parents the world was full of dangers and temptations. I was allowed to walk to the beach alone but I was forbidden from other places, like the cinema on a Sunday or Catholic churches. There was a sharp demarcation between nature (good) and culture (bad). After I left Australia to live first in New Zealand and then England, I was often amused by people telling me they could never even visit Australia because it was so dangerous, with all those deadly snakes and spiders and sharks. When you grow up there, though, these are just a given – you walk through the bush taking care where you plant your feet, you never put your hand in a tree hollow or under a rock, you don't swim at the beach at dawn or dusk.

I was always cautious but I was never terrified in those surroundings. Instead, I was afraid of things closer to home: the dark; losing my parents; a monstrous face I saw one night in a patterned veneer door of a wardrobe in an unfamiliar bedroom. As an adolescent, however, the list of things I feared grew steadily as my frame of experience widened. There seemed so many dangers and, for some reason, growing up female made one especially vulnerable. There was so much that I apparently needed to be wary of – the children of non-believing neighbours, the streets after dark, popular music, makeup – that it often seemed easiest to assume everything was dangerous because if I guessed wrong my parents would be *very disappointed* in me.

At the same time, though, they were powerless to protect me from the daily dangers that caused me so much anxiety (and which, to be fair, it would never have occurred to me to tell them about): the casual bullying from the older girls if you sat on the wrong seat on the school bus (or even sat in the wrong way on your seat); the offhand sexual abuse to which some boys in my class subjected the girls, lingering around a flight of steps that we had to descend every day. As the girls walked down, the boys would take the opportunity to ascend and, as the two groups crossed on the steps, the boys would 'feel us up', in that awful euphemistic vernacular of the time. The ridiculously short uniforms we wore then made it all too easy for a hot, clutching hand to be thrust between your legs. While the boys laughed uproariously at their own daring, never tiring of this 'game', we girls never thought to tell a teacher. We barely talked about it even among ourselves and never named it as a violation; it was so ordinary, no need to make a fuss about it, just part of the normal day in a large co-ed high school.

✲

When I was approaching 15 an inspirational poster hung in our lime-green kitchen, depicting a desert scene with a single flowering cactus in the foreground. *Bloom where you are planted* was the caption. This kitchen where I was daily entreated to bloom was in a small, dark, terraced house on a busy road in inner-city Sydney. We had just moved back to the city so that my father could have a mid-life career change: he was now training to become a clergyman. Instead of bush behind my house there was only the brick wall of the neighbours' house, with a window at which they could be seen washing up, overlooking our small courtyard with a single frangipani tree. It was the tenth kitchen of my life so far. My family was always being transplanted. A change of scene – a new address, a new career – was the solution to any problem, it seemed.

And yet, in many ways, I did bloom there. After the limitations of a small beach town, I thrived on the cosmopolitan nature of Newtown, only just beginning gentrification and still rough around the edges. We now lived very near the university I would attend in a few years' time, so I could observe the boho sophistication of the students as they walked past my house on their way to pubs or cafés. I tasted baklava and falafel for the first time. At my Sydney girls' school, I was no longer groped by boys or bullied for being smart. I discovered books, films and music that – long before the internet – had not penetrated the cultural wastelands of small-town Australia. Change had made me ill that first year back in the city but eventually it made me flourish. It was not just an escape from the country but an escape into a different kind of life, albeit one that required careful negotiation around what was permitted, where you could go, what you could read, what you could say. One had to pay close attention, like a careful reader. And I was always a very careful reader.

4.

Everything
is
broken

Literature offered escape and possibility but it also presented clear
plot lines and a sense of consequences. *If 'x' happens, then 'y' is sure
to follow.* A life spent reading means that I tend to think in narrative
patterns. It's how I make sense of things. Everything happens for a
reason in novels.

With hindsight, nineteenth-century narratives may not have been
the best preparation for life in the twenty-first century, although
a sheltered upbringing as the adolescent daughter of a clergyman
in the late twentieth century is closer to the world of *Wives and
Daughters* than you might assume. As a young adult, for instance, I was
a weekly attender at a church where Jane Eyre's expressions of female
independence would still have been condemned as *unbiblical* (the
ultimate and unanswerable charge), over a hundred and fifty years after
the poor, plain governess first uttered them.

It was probably *Little Women* that started it all. My mother had a
hardcover copy that I read over and over (although the companion

volume of *Good Wives* did not engage my affections in the same way). Then, in Year Seven, my best friend and I had discovered *Gone with the Wind* (a narrative *about* the nineteenth century, at least) and we both read it three times in a year, an almost daily weight we suffered in our schoolbags so we could read it on the bus. My red hardcover copy (also my mother's) fell apart from such rough treatment. It's troubling now to think how much of my ambivalence about female autonomy can probably be traced back to my early obsession with those contrasting American classics, *Little Women* and *Gone with the Wind*. My mother was the fiction reader in the family, and although she would later be uneasy about my desire to study literature at university (*people lose their faith at university*, she warned) I knew she was pleased that I shared her love of novels (although I drew the line at Georgette Heyer).

In childhood, re-reading books had been a necessity in a small beach town where the public library was a dingy ante-room off the foyer of the local hall. My mother and I visited weekly while my father waited outside in the car with my fractious baby sister. If there were four people in the library, plus the librarian behind a modest desk squeezed into a corner, it was uncomfortably crowded. Despite its small dimensions the local library still observed the conventions of far grander institutions: borrowers perused the shelves with studied concentration and in total silence. Any essential conversation had to be whispered – regardless of whatever raucous event was taking place in the hall outside – and the date stamping of books was like a gunshot in a phone box.

Books lined the walls on three sides of the room, with the Junior section right by the door as you entered. There was no window so the door was kept open and, in my memory, it was always draughty and cold as I stood scanning the shelves, hoping to stumble on a treasure I had overlooked on previous visits, like a new Joan G. Robinson novel. I quickly exhausted the offerings of the Junior section but was not yet permitted to move onto the larger Adult Fiction section, so many visits ended in disappointment. I remember borrowing *The Pickwick Papers* – shelved as a children's book – more than once. It baffled me as a nine- or ten-year-old; I didn't make much headway with it and it remains the Dickens-I-never-finished.

The high-school library – a vast and airy space after the shelved broom cupboard to which I was accustomed – was a revelation in Year Seven, freeing me from the constraints of Junior Fiction. After a brief segue into science fiction (of *The Day of the Triffids* ilk) and Agatha Christie it was on to Jane Austen, and I have been reading nineteenth-century British fiction ever since.

I especially liked characters who felt deeply and struggled with the conflict between social responsibility and individual freedom. 'Yearning' is not a word you hear a lot now but nineteenth-century novels are full of it, and that was a big part of their appeal for me. In late high school I discovered Thomas Hardy and spent a few years imaginatively inhabiting Hardy's green melancholic world, which exactly matched my prevailing mood of gloomy angst and unacknowledged desires.

It was not just the nineteenth-century stories, though, but the attention to everyday life that I loved in these novels: what people wore, what they ate, the rooms where they sat, the landscapes they traversed. I'm the same with movies: I'm always completely caught up in the opening scenarios of ordinariness, before the major event happens that jolts the characters out of their mundane routines and propels the plot – the appearance of the mysterious stranger, the discovery of the dead body, the alien invasion – and I often wish the whole movie could be about the ordinary stuff, without the apocalypse, so I could just keep watching people going about their daily lives, cooking their meals, working at their desks, drinking coffee, going shopping.

Victorian novels also presented me with a natural environment that seemed to come alive on the page, even though it was totally foreign to me: the woodlands and apple orchards where Giles Winterborne toiled; the hidden pool to which poor Hetty Sorrel was drawn on her lonely pilgrimage; the quiet lanes and churchyards where the Woman in White lingered. When I discovered that some readers skipped over such passages to hurry on the plot, I was mystified: what were they reading for if not to immerse themselves in the alternative reality of an imagined landscape? I would often read such descriptive passages twice before continuing on with the thread of the story.

It is perhaps not surprising, then, that teaching nineteenth-century British literature became my profession, a career choice that, in turn, eventually brought me to a university in southeast England. Here, I thought, I could immerse myself in the landscape of the novels I knew so well. Charles Dickens was a pervasive presence in Kent (so much so that one house has a sign declaring *Charles Dickens Did Not Live Here*); Wilkie Collins used to live in a nearby coastal town; Joseph Conrad's house was in a village a few miles away; and Jane Austen started what would become *Pride and Prejudice* in the stately home in our neighbouring village, where we would regularly go in the summer to walk the shady lime avenue or sit in the walled garden full of peonies and climbing roses.

Committing to the 'full English' experience, my husband and I bought a sixteenth-century thatched longhouse in an East Kent village, straight out of an episode of *Escape to the Country*. The first night we spent in the house we awoke to a thick layer of unseasonal snow on the thatch. We didn't know it at the time but this April snow marked the dramatic end to a record-breaking long, cold winter. The late arrival of spring our first year in England meant that everything seemed to bud and bloom at once, overlapping to create a riot of colour and greenery like a speeded-up, time-lapse photography sequence. From the first crocuses to the prolific summer roses, our garden had an abundance of flowers and fragrance, attracting birds and butterflies. If you stood in the vegetable patch you could see the village church spire, framed by fruit trees at the end of the garden. I could lie in bed at night and regularly hear the hooting of a tawny owl.

Pretty soon into my new life in England, however, it became apparent to me that the narrative I had imagined for this phase of my life (*then I moved to England, where I enjoyed both professional acclaim and gracious living*) was not proceeding according to plan. I frequently felt waves of homesickness for New Zealand that were a longing for landscape as much as a sense of profound dislocation from the place where – too late – I now felt I really belonged. I remember, that first summer in Kent, washing up at the sink one evening, looking out at the lavender light that seemed to make the pink blooms on the climbing rose outside the kitchen window glow in the dusk. The beauty of the scene provided no comfort. I was listening to Thom Yorke sing *Guess that's it / I've made my bed / I'll lie in it,* and weeping over the dishes.

I may have hoped for a happy ending to my English pastoral but I knew all too well that there were lots of other possible endings, like those where the protagonist suffered and then probably died, or at least was *thwarted*, another great Victorian theme. Like one of Hardy's tragic protagonists, I had made a wrong choice, failed to recognise where I really belonged, instead setting off on a path that promised much but resulted in bitter failure. Everything happens for a reason, but not necessarily one that results in happiness. So instead of thinking, *this is just a bad run, I need time to adjust, circumstances have taken an unfortunate turn,* I began to fear that bad times defined me and my story. And that it was all my fault. *Despair is a form of certainty,* writes the essayist Rebecca Solnit, *certainty that the future will be a lot like the present, or will decline from it.*

In an attempt to make sense of what was happening to me, I started to explore the following narrative options in my head – on a sliding scale from the prosaic to the melodramatic:

> It's career burnout.
> It's a mid-life crisis.
> I have lost my way.
> England has broken me.

And I began to descend into a very dark place. *The distinguishing mental features of melancholia,* Freud writes,

> are a profoundly painful dejection, cessation of interest in the outside world, loss of the capacity to love, inhibition of all activity, and a lowering of self-regarding feelings to a degree that finds utterance in self-reproaches and self-revilings, and culminates in a delusional expectation of punishment.

Self-reviling perfectly summed up my ruminations at this time. More than self-criticism, self-reviling involves attacking the self *in an angry, abusive or insulting manner,* as the OED has it. Deriving from the Anglo-Norman *revilir,* revile is also related to the Italian *ravvilire* which, in a now obsolete meaning, had the sense of weakening the resistance of a person. I was wearing myself away, from the inside, with my raging recriminations. I offered myself no comfort for the pain I was experiencing. I had instigated this move across the planet, uprooting my family from a comfortable life in Dunedin, in my quest for career achievement. I was to blame. I could even see the escalation of my OCD as an attempt to punish myself. You've moved to Europe for an exciting new life? Too bad you won't be able to enjoy it; inhibition of all activity will see to that. You'll be stuck at home most of the time, immobilised by fear, turning down repeated opportunities to travel, whether across the country or the Continent, and to experience new things.

I lost interest in my work and my house and even my family. I cut myself off from people. Nothing gave me pleasure, other than my dog and my chardonnay. Severe insomnia was a nightly event. Performing normal tasks became impossible. My powers of concentration evaporated and my work productivity diminished to a point where I was pretty useless, as well as hopeless. After the Scandi-blanc therapist, I had no confidence in seeking any other help or treatment.

There was, however, a basic contradiction in my story at this point. If one believed that life was fundamentally, irrevocably, meaningless and bleak and that's just how it was, one might simply trundle on, resignedly. But if one seriously considered opting out, as I did repeatedly after moving to England, it might be because one thinks that life could, *should*, have meaning, purpose, pleasure, connection. In the absence of that, life becomes intolerable to the point where death seems a viable choice. To paraphrase David Hume, I believe that *no woman ever threw away life, while it was worth keeping.*

If I contemplated suicide, then, did that mean I was actually an optimist at heart? According to the Romanian philosopher E.M. Cioran, *Only optimists commit suicide, the optimists who can no longer be … optimists.* If I refused to accept as a life one where I felt dogged by despair and depression every day was that not, in a perverse way, life-affirming? On the other hand, if I found daily life unbearably painful but continued anyway was that, too, in fact a gesture of hope, of optimism beyond reasonable doubt?

When Virginia Woolf, at 15, asked *how is one to live in such a world?* it was not (or not merely) a gloomy presage of death. (I often find the biographers of famous suicides bleaker than their subjects – everything relentlessly points to death.) Woolf's question also expressed a desire *to live*, if one only knew how. And, yes, I know I'm back to obsessing about famous dead women but they have left a record of their thoughts, desires and fears in a way that unremarked women unfortunately have not. At the same time, their madness (if that is what it was) is the most ordinary thing about women like Woolf and Plath. Their literary genius marked them as extraordinary, but their struggle to find meaning and pleasure in daily life is what made them human, one of us.

The choice that Woolf and Plath each made when life had become unsustainable seemed to me to articulate – to the bitter end – a sense that life could, should, be otherwise. In their final acts of despair there was still evident a sense of love, a wish to connect with others, as Woolf's suicide note makes heartbreakingly clear. (*What I want to say is I owe all the happiness of my life to you*, she wrote to Leonard.) Even Plath's choice was in some way a gesture of love: to reach the point where one felt so broken that one's children would be better off without one's presence in their lives is irredeemably sad, but it is a kind of gift – giving one's children the gift of a life not weighed down by the presence of a sad, suffering, not-good-enough mother as a daily exemplar. It's not a great gift, admittedly, but it is not simply an act of unspeakable selfishness – abandoning one's children – that it is so often judged to be.

What kind of coherence does suicide give a life? asks the philosopher Simon Critchley: *Suicide might grant life coherence, but only by robbing it of complexity by viewing it through the instant of one's death.* It's true that, much as I might decry the ghoulishness of literary biographers, I too was reading these famous women's lives, the meaning of their lives, through the prism of their voluntary deaths. Part of suicide's seductive appeal for me was the coherence of death, not merely marking the end of struggle and suffering but achieving the kind of closure that could not be matched even by a great nineteenth-century novel. *That* is how the story ends and, after that, no more drama, no more danger.

🙟

As my mood became ever blacker and bleaker, I lost the ability to read novels at all. I found it near impossible to enthuse undergraduates about the delights of the triple-decker Victorian novels I had set them to read, when these very books confronted me accusingly, unread on my bedside table. I used to regard it as one of the keenest pleasures of my job that I *had* to re-read classic novels before teaching them each year so they would be fresh in my mind. Now I found myself in stale, overheated seminar rooms trying to encourage bored students (furtively looking down at the smartphones on their laps under the table) to persist with the next 400 pages of this week's novel, failing to convince even myself that this was a worthwhile or achievable task. Could they tell? I'm sure they could. They may not know much about George Eliot's philosophy but undergraduates have excellent bullshit detectors, in my experience.

There is nothing like a crypt-like seminar room to make you feel a profoundly painful dejection and a cessation of interest in the outside world. Standing at the front of a classroom is a vulnerable position in which to put yourself at the best of times, and no place to be when the point of life eludes you. On top of that, to have lost the capacity to love literature – or anything else that I used to love – marked an alienation from myself I can't really describe. I have always felt at home on a university campus, but now I could be in the midst of an ordinary day – sitting in a meeting, walking to a class – and I would suddenly feel outside myself, not knowing what was holding me in place, holding me in *this* place, as if I could float away, untethered, without anything grounding me. My real life felt unreal, as if I had left myself behind on the other side of the world while a shadow self kept up appearances here.

Since I couldn't read novels (and, at my worst, even reading a newspaper article through to the end became impossible), my compulsion for narrative had to find an alternative outlet. I became addicted to those TV property programmes where people want to change their life and start afresh, in a new location, with a new home. Will they get *the feeling* when they walk in the front door of the next house? Will they find the project that will allow them to build a new life? Will their new windows ever be delivered?

The hope and optimism of those TV people who wanted a new adventure, who didn't want *to look back in 10 or 15 years and wish we had done it*, was compelling and bewildering in equal parts. I envied their confidence that an architect-designed, eco-sustainable building could make them happy forever. Or that they could move to a Mediterranean village where they would pick up the language and become part of a community, uprooting from the only place they had ever lived in exchange for somewhere they had perhaps holidayed for two weeks a year but that felt like home. I recognised the wishful thinking that associated 'anywhere but here' with a better life. If I work too hard here, *there* it will be easier; if my relationships lack intimacy, *there* they will be reinvigorated; if my life lacks purpose here, *there* it will be meaningful; if I don't find pleasure in daily life here, *there* I will find contentment. Who could deny the appeal of such a utopian narrative?

Meanwhile, I could not shake the feeling that I would never be my normal self – my *real* self? – as long as I lived in England. I felt like I was in exile on another planet to which I would never adjust. I wanted to go home. I had visited Britain many times, spent extended periods of research leave there, had good friends dotted across the country who I looked forward to seeing more regularly now they were just a train ride away. I had a job with new challenges and colleagues I admired. Maybe I just needed more time to settle. But every night, between around 2 and 5am, I knew that life on these terms was not sustainable.

How is one to live in such a world?

I had no idea.

5.

This
will
restore
your
creativity

Thus spake the cheerful German psychiatrist, trying to sell me on doubling the dosage of my medication. My previous experience of antipodean psychiatrists had been limited to men who were socially inept or misanthropic (sometimes both at once), so Dr Z was a pleasant surprise, despite his insistence that he greet me with what he described as *a therapeutic handshake* (and similarly insisted that we repeat the ritual on my departure). In response to his inquiries, I described the 'suicidal ideation' (as the side-effects pamphlet in my box of tablets put it) that had plagued me when I had started the medication a few months previously, having finally braved a visit to the GP for a prescription. The constant thoughts of knives and pills, the lure of the bluebell wood as a possible final location, I had kept entirely to myself until now. I added that I thought this side-effect was usually confined to children and young adults taking this drug and he replied, *You must be young at heart!*

The goal of my treatment, according to Dr Z, was to achieve the ability to encounter the train, the supermarket checkout, the pharmacy, and tell myself *it'll be fine*. The ability to move on to the next task, without a second thought about the consequences of contact, ingestion or proximity. *It'll be fine*, he repeated, with a rather theatrical shrug for emphasis.

Not a very grand conclusion. No great mystery to be unravelled, then. No life-changing epiphany on the meaning of existence. Just getting on with the mundanities of daily life and saying, *meh. Big deal.*

I wasn't sure how I felt about this goal. Of course I longed to live without fear and anxiety, to dispel the dreadful power that I had invested in the banal. But I didn't see it as ideal to no longer pay close attention to the ordinary. I just didn't want that attention to result in crippling terror.

My referral to Dr Z had come about as a result of a further deterioration in my ability to concentrate or to complete work. I couldn't cover up my lack of productivity any longer. Usually scrupulously punctual, I was forgetting deadlines and neglecting administrative duties because I couldn't focus on the complexity of the tasks involved. I started to sit at the back of the room during weekly research seminars because I would invariably fall asleep. I slept through most of a conference I was hosting. And if paperwork and meetings were a challenge, the kind of creative thinking that was essential for producing research had eluded me for some time. So Dr Z's conviction that a double dosage would restore a part of me that I had always felt was central to who I am – the ability to think, read, imagine – was a welcome idea, if I could believe him.

A few days later I received a copy of the report that Dr Z had sent to my occupational health counsellor at the university. A strange document, it seemed more like a letter of recommendation from the 1950s (*Thank you very much for referring this pleasant lady to us here at Mindwell. It has been a pleasure seeing her on Thursday 24 September*) than a clinical psychiatric report. More jarring, though, was seeing my illness spelled out in black and white (*In diagnostic terms she is clearly suffering from both OCD and major depression*). The 'major' was something of a surprise. To be assessed in this way – after three months on medication – was simultaneously a validation of my symptoms and grounds for further despair.

'Major depression' would, however, provide some explanation for my chronic insomnia. During the workday I might succumb to drowsiness if forced to sit still and listen passively for any extended period, but at night I could not fall asleep, stay asleep, or sleep deeply. I never dreamed any more. I thought I would go mad from the sheer tedium of wakefulness if nothing else. All the guides to good sleep hygiene warn against looking at computer screens in bed, but watching TV online on my laptop was often the only thing that kept me from running screaming into the night. That and the comfort of a bowl of cereal at 3am.

And always the constant looping thoughts, like a bad haiku, through the night: *It's career burnout / England has broken me / I have lost my way*.

At one point my sympathetic osteopath (who was treating me for a frozen shoulder) gave me a 'sleep ball' – the size and shape of a flattened tennis ball, covered in grey felted wool and filled with lavender and hops – to see if it helped.

It worked a treat. Just not for me.

The first night I placed it under my pillow out of sight – to give the soporific aromas a few hours to permeate my pillow and work their magic – but later that evening when I was preparing for bed I found the sleep ball had disappeared. On a hunch, I checked the dog's bed in the next room and, sure enough, there she was, curled up in a deep sleep, with my sleep ball between her front paws. I, by contrast, woke at midnight after a short doze and thereafter heard the village clock chime one, two, three and four before drifting off around 5am for a couple of hours.

❦

Psychoanalyst D. W. Winnicott described depression as *unaliveness*, a mood of *deadness, heaviness, darkness*. It's a clumsy term, *unaliveness*, but an evocative one. Think of what makes you feel alive, what gives you vitality, and then think of the absence of all those qualities. You're not dead – you get up each day and drag yourself around the daily routines, or as many of them as you can still manage – but it's not much of a life. You're un-alive. Winnicott's *deadness, heaviness, darkness*, plus Freud's *self-revilings* encapsulated my experience of depression at this time. When I did not have the energy to work I somehow always had the energy for plenty of self-reviling.

The leaden state I was experiencing was something I know that others with depression have described too. *On the ground floor of depression*, writes Mark Rice-Oxley,

> you are just holding out for some respite, a bit of joined-up sleep, an end to the anxiety pangs and the endless, ludicrous chatter of rumination. You tell yourself, if I recover I promise I will not want so much, need so much, do so much, aspire to so much. It will be enough for me just to be myself again, without all the horror. Just me, a person, bumbling around, marveling at flowers and skies and the changing of the seasons and the power of the sea.

It's like living underwater or inside a tunnel – life is going on elsewhere, where people are managing to have fun and also pay their bills on time. You can catch a glimpse of them and their world, you may even vaguely recall living there yourself, but you can't get to it. A numbing inertia robs you of the capacity to be either convivial or responsible. And the desire for recovery becomes simply a wish to live a quiet life without desperation.

It might have seemed like I was idling the day away at home, staring out the window, making too many cups of coffee, picking up and putting down books without reading them, but there was a dark filter between me and the outside world, trapping me in an airless bubble alone with my thoughts of despair, failure, futility, so that by the end of the day I would be exhausted by their weight and darkness. And there were a couple of nights when the only reason I resolved to go on living the next day was the thought of my daughter back in New Zealand learning of my fate by phone call.

Above all, I couldn't understand why this was happening to me *now*? Hadn't I achieved a long-held ambition: to become a professor in my field at an English university? Darian Leader, a psychoanalyst influenced by Freud's essay called 'Those Wrecked by Success', has speculated that sometimes depression can be triggered after achieving a much-desired goal. *When there is no longer anything to attain*, Leader writes, *we feel the presence of a void at the core of our lives*. On my first day in the new job in England I had sat in my dark, cold and bare office and cried. Aspiration, energy, desire, even curiosity, had begun to ebb away almost from the moment I had landed at Heathrow. After those early months, as my unhappiness and homesickness morphed almost imperceptibly into depression and my contamination phobia ratcheted up to extreme levels, I stopped crying. Un-alive people don't cry. What's the point? Crying requires too much energy. You will eventually have to stop crying, and everything will be unchanged from its current shitty state. So why bother starting to weep?

It sounded counter-intuitive but it felt like success had robbed me of the will to live, or at least had presented me with a life that I no longer recognised as something I wanted. As Adam Phillips has wryly observed: *There is … nothing like success to show us that we are not quite who we think we are.*

6.

Tell me about your journey

The next stop on the treatment round was an appointment with Mr H, recommended to me as a therapist who wove literature and philosophy into his therapeutic approach. I thought he might help me to gain some insight into my 'mid-life issues', which, as I put it in my email to him, I wanted to explore without focusing exclusively on my depression and OCD in the first instance. I had a hunch that my symptoms were telling me that I needed to live otherwise, find a new direction, but I felt clueless to figure out what that might look like as long as I wallowed in my own misery. I didn't feel able to face a form of therapy as confronting as that offered by the Scandi-blanc therapist but I wanted to give some attention to the bigger picture and figure out where I should be, what I should be doing, who I should be.

Almost immediately I knew he was a mistake.

When I entered the large sitting-room in his Georgian house, full of that distinctive and rather suffocating smell of old books, he offered me a seat and a glass of water. I sank down into a too-soft red plush sofa and declined the water. He insisted. *You will need it. You will be doing a lot of talking.* And he left the room before I could demur, soon returning with a tumbler of water that he placed on a low table in front of me.

Within the first half hour of the 90-minute appointment he had made reference to Martin Heidegger, Maurice Merleau-Ponty, Percy Bysshe Shelley, Samuel Beckett, James Joyce, Walt Whitman, Sigmund Freud. He also explained to me at length that most people thought *The Great Gatsby* (one of his favourite books) was a love story but it was really about the existential crisis of modern man. I wanted to say *Books can be about more than one thing* but didn't. I also didn't know what the hell *The Great Gatsby* had to do with my situation. He spoke almost constantly and seemed uninterested in me other than as a type. *Depressives often feel,* he would commence. *Anxious people usually …*

I sat nodding, rarely speaking, rarely being invited to speak, as he seemed to already know all about me. In exasperation, at one point I interjected almost randomly, *Do you ever refer to women writers?* Looking offended, he immediately mentioned Plath and Woolf, before leaping up from his chair to pull a Siri Hustvedt book off his shelf to show me. He offered to lend it to me.

By the end of the session there had been no opportunity to mention my mid-life issues. He hadn't asked and I had felt powerless to turn the conversation towards them. I wrote him a cheque, effectively having paid him to talk about himself and his thoughts, and left. My glass of water remained untouched on the table.

᠅

My own choice of therapist having proved a disaster, I moved on to the psychologist recommended by Occupational Health. Unlike Mr H, this psychologist seemed to show a genuine interest in me, rather than just my symptoms. He was big on the *life is a journey* metaphor but I could buy into that because of my own attachment to narratives. *Tell me about your journey. We want to make sense of where you are today in terms of your past journey and where you are going.* He must have said this in every session we had.

The main reason I initially warmed to the Journeyman, though, was that he fully supported my desire to return to New Zealand. He

understood that whatever he could offer me was a poor substitute
for the place where I felt at home. He did not make me feel that
his task was simply to restore me to health so I could become a
fully productive employee of the university again as soon as possible.
Indeed, both he and Dr Z, immigrants themselves, seemed to take
it for granted that living in the UK could be a soul-destroying
experience.

Before the end of the first session, the Journeyman ruled out a
standard course of cognitive behavioural therapy (the ostensible reason
for my referral from Occupational Health) as unsuitable for me in
my current circumstances. We were going to work on my existential
journey. My toes may have curled a little at this but I was comforted
by the fact that, at the end of the first session, he asked *Are you safe?* –
as if he really meant it.

In subsequent sessions, however, the Journeyman started to break
out the whiteboard and draw diagrams to explain things to me. The
old brain and the new brain. Adrenalin and cortisol. Survival versus
progress. My heart sank. The Journeyman talked a lot about the
importance of feeling things *in your blood and your bones*, about what
was *good for your soul,* but he stood at the whiteboard mansplaining
every week, even encouraging me to take notes if I wanted.

I didn't.

I came to the end of the road with the Journeyman after six of
my nine scheduled sessions. In the sixth session, when he pressed me
to provide *a synopsis* of my journey narrative so far, it occurred to me
that if I was going to be constructing narratives I would rather do that
at home on my laptop than in his office. I could tell my own story, in
my own way. And then I would also be spared the easy-listening radio
that always seemed to be playing George Michael singing 'I'm Your
Man' while I sat in the shabby waiting room beside the staff kitchen.

The most valuable thing I gained from my sessions with the
Journeyman was his insistence on the power of narrative. It spurred
me to start writing, and to begin to imagine a life where I might
spend even more time writing. Either Dr Z's higher drug dosage had
restored my creativity, or the Journeyman's encouragement to dwell
on narratives had sunk in. In any case, I felt a growing compulsion to
write and to read the stories of others who had been along a similar

path. From struggling to read anything longer than a book review, or taking forever to read undemanding novels that I didn't really approve of (all with the word *Girl* in their titles, oddly), I found an increased capacity to sit engrossed with more challenging books for longer periods of time. The fog seemed to be lifting from my brain, even if I was still plagued by contamination phobia and OCD. When I managed to sleep, I was dreaming vividly and frequently. I mulled over memories and ideas on my daily walks and rushed to write them down when I reached home. They were just fragments, paragraphs at most, but they reminded me of the pleasures of writing, of the kind of calm, unlike any other, that writing can bestow, one where you feel fully alert and at ease at the same time.

7.

Closer
to
fine

But I couldn't always stay at home writing. The outside world still impinged, with all its potential dangers and germs, its commitments and obligations.

For a contamination phobic, it is extremely difficult to filter experience, to distinguish between the terrifying, the merely unpleasant, the tedious, or the not-particularly-anything task or encounter. The boundary between self and world seems so porous, so vulnerable to attack, that every undertaking is charged with significance. If everything is momentous, though, then nothing is truly significant. The risk of sensory overload – feeling constantly bombarded by potentially threatening stimuli, always monitoring for danger or a breach in the barrier against a perilous world – easily leads to emotional shutdown, a disconnection from anything truly meaningful or imbued with positive, rather than negative, feeling.

As children, we (supposedly) learn to filter experience, to distinguish the important from the trivial, the life-threatening from the mundane. Freud called it *the reality principle*: our gradual lesson in adjusting to the vicissitudes of life in order to avoid being overwhelmed by sensation or experience, fear or desire. Children eventually learn that they can't stop to wonder at everything, or weep over every hurt, or recoil from everything unfamiliar if they are to avoid missing out on the next thing, or being suffocated by life, or neglected by those whose comfort they need. *The wide glare of the children's day*, writes Robert Graves in his poem 'The Cool Web' (with more than a passing nod to Wordsworth), grows dimmer as we mature. If we are to become adults who function efficiently in a workaday world, we necessarily – and inevitably – lose the intensity of childhood experience, Graves lamented:

> Children are dumb to say how hot the day is,
> How hot the scent is of the summer rose,
>
> ...
>
> But we have speech, to chill the angry day,
> And speech, to dull the rose's cruel scent.

As an obsessive-compulsive phobic, I still had a childlike intensity of feeling when exposed to anything dreadful. Despite the fact that books and *the cool web of language* were my trade, I had never succeeded in finding a way to diminish the dread through words alone. How to decrease the fear without losing all capacity for feeling in response to the world around me was a mystery. Others I observed going about their daily business did not seem to convey any sense of being dogged by an existential threat from buses, post offices or small children. Had they grasped reality in a way that I hadn't? What was their secret?

For me, cities were especially overwhelming – so many people! – because of the myriad threats they posed from the moment one arrived: crowded train platforms, coughing strangers, sticky rubber handrails on escalators, ominous stains on the pavement. And yet I would see people around me chatting with friends, or striding purposefully to their next engagement, as if they did not have a care in the world. In a city like London I felt porous to the point of transparency: I couldn't feel any protective margin between myself and the barrage of sensations – the smells, noise, touch. City people seemed to have a different sense of personal space and bodily parameters: they came too close, and seemed cavalier about what they touched and how many others had done so before them. They exuded an air of entitlement, as if the city was simply there for them to inhabit, to enjoy if they could, or just make the best of. But I always felt exposed and powerless, and my only defence was therefore to remain in a state of hypersensitivity, in a futile attempt to anticipate all danger.

ᴡ

To be overly sensitive used to be attributed to 'delicate nerves'. Such delicacy was typically coded as feminine (my mother would often say she was *feeling a bit nervy today*), and seen as an expression of weakness. In the eighteenth century, though, the nerves had been understood as a direct link between body and mind: when they vibrated (as they were thought to do), something was up. It was believed that jangling, tingling or vibrating nerves could be a sign of impending physical or mental collapse, or they could signal a sympathetic response to someone else's suffering. As a child, and knowing absolutely nothing about eighteenth-century literature, I was well acquainted with nervousness as a bad feeling to be avoided, a lot like fear, but to be sensitive was a much more confusing idea. I would hear someone referred to as *a sensitive child* and would be unsure whether to pity or envy them. Were they special? Or unwell? I couldn't figure it out. But it seemed important somehow.

When I was six, I was thrilled one day to find that – unaccountably – I had been adopted by a sophisticated group of older girls (aged eight or nine) who I had watched playing out complicated scenarios under the canopy of the coral trees in one corner of the schoolyard. The large exposed tree roots formed the rooms or settings for their various role-playing games and I used to linger, enthralled by their lunchtime performances. Now, given the unexpected opportunity, I threw myself fully into their impromptu dramas and won the approval of the girl who stage-managed these games. Taking me aside in confidence one lunchtime, she pointed out another girl in the group – quiet, plain, prone to tears – and informed me that she was *sensitive* so we all needed to be careful how we treated her. I was flattered to be the recipient of this confidential information (after all, the sensitive girl was two years older than me but I was assumed to be as capable of watching out for her as the other, older girls). At the same time, though, I was envious that I had not been singled out (although I was still not entirely sure what 'sensitive' meant, other than teary). The sensitive girl was clearly special in some way – even though she mostly looked glum – and, because of this, the other girls I admired paid extra attention to her. They did not exclude her on account of being a crybaby, which would have been the more typical playground stratagem, but took care of her, adapting roles to suit her downcast demeanour so that she could still be included in the game.

I wanted to be sensitive too but, for now, I wanted to show that I was worthy of the ringleader's confidence, that I had the maturity of an eight-year-old when it came to caring for others. So I approached the sensitive girl and said, *I know you are sensitive but that's okay, we will look out for you.*

She promptly burst into tears.

The leader girl, having observed all this, was furious. *What have you done?* she said. *You don't TELL a sensitive person that they are sensitive!*

Having thus demonstrated my childish insensitivity, I was instantly expelled from the group and forced to return to the other six-year-olds, playing rowdily in another part of the playground (but not rowdily enough to be unaware of my fall from grace).

Be careful what you wish for.

Now in England I experienced heightened sensitivity on a daily basis – I couldn't keep the world at bay. The outside wouldn't stay outside but permeated the bulwark that I tried to keep between myself and an invasive world of dirt and germs. I always had antennae alert for any possible dangers or source of threat – smells, sounds, the feel of objects I touched, the awareness of the air that I breathed. I couldn't block out other people's conversations, and an internal alarm would go off if I overheard – or thought I heard – words like *illness, sick, off-colour, poorly, 24-hour thing, some kind of bug*, etc. Attempting to police the barriers between the world and me was exhausting.

So committing to a day trip to catch up with an Australian friend who was on a brief visit to London was an undertaking that loomed large over my week. The Occupational Health counsellor thought it was *an important step in my recovery* and was full of helpful advice about how to manage it (*take disposable gloves, change seats in the train if you feel unsure of the health of passengers in your vicinity*). Hearing her suggestions made me newly aware of how ridiculous my condition was, a condition that reduced me, a middle-aged, educated woman, to receiving – needing? – this kind of advice.

Thursday came around too quickly. I took a long time getting ready in order to distract my thoughts from dwelling on the enormity of the task ahead – a train to London, lunch in a restaurant – but proceeded as if I was actually going ahead with the plan, telling myself I could back out at any point and send my friend a pathetic text, *Sorry, couldn't make it after all.*

I was surprised, however, to find myself on the train and not feeling too overwhelmed with fear. I had checked my seat carefully before sitting down (reasonably clean, no suspicious or disturbing rubbish). I was a little anxious about the woman coughing directly behind me, but I listened to my iPod to drown out the sound and concentrated on the autumnal scenery flashing by. Distant pheasants in a green meadow framed by trees of russet, gold and ochre. A solitary horse-rider. Flocks of white seagulls wheeling over chocolate-brown fields, freshly furrowed. My shoulders relaxed.

I met my friend at St Pancras and we walked to the Italian restaurant I had booked. I think I talked non-stop. After lunch we walked back to the station, past pedestrians hunched against a light November drizzle that made the streets slick. My friend was returning to the British Library for the rest of the afternoon, but I went to wait for my train. It was cancelled but it was okay. I didn't panic or catastrophise. I waited alone with the ever-growing throng: the next train would now have to accommodate all the passengers who would normally have been spread over two services. When the train arrived, I managed to find a seat, read the *LRB*, and travelled home. The man sitting next to me applied hand sanitiser liberally before settling down to read his hardcover adventure novel.

It was fine.

8.

Fretwork

While I had been adjusting to medication, navigating the therapy circuit and starting to write this story, however, much else had changed. My husband and I, both equally disenchanted with life in England, had begun to plan an exit strategy. He applied for a job back in New Zealand. We put the thatched house up for sale.

Two-and-a-half years after we had first moved to England, therefore, I was living alone, renting a cottage in a small market town not far from our old village, which I now drove through every day on my way to work, past our old house that had sold quickly. My husband and son – and the dog – had all flown home to New Zealand; the North Island this time.

My life felt in limbo. Sometimes I felt disoriented when I left my cottage and saw Tudor houses facing me on the other side of the narrow street, and was surprised to discover I was still in England because most of the time I was thinking about New Zealand, imagining being there, and vicariously experiencing my family's move to Matakana. My husband Skyped to show me the sea view from the verandah of our new house, to sort out the furniture placement, to select paint colours.

Continuing in my career would mean staying in England, at least in the short term (the academic job market in New Zealand seemed to be ever-contracting), but I counted down the days till I was due to join my family at the end of the year, when the Christmas break would be followed by a term's study leave. In the meantime, I still had many weeks of term to drag through as the year declined into winter and the nights drew in.

My relationship with routine during this time was contradictory. Some routines provided me with a sense of reassuring continuity – we obsessive-compulsive phobics are creatures of habit because habit feels like control and control feels safe – while others required a kind of optimism (*there will be a future so paying your bills regularly is important*) that I couldn't muster and therefore often neglected. Most days I managed to force myself to take some exercise and go to work, but other mundane tasks, even opening the mail, seemed pointless. I shopped regularly at the supermarket (thanks to copious amounts of hand sanitiser), although the meals I prepared were increasingly simple and unvaried, just a means to an end. Other forms of shopping that became pressing (a bread knife, a lamp socket) went unattempted. I've never been exactly conscientious about domestic maintenance chores, but I used to like cooking and buying stuff. Now I couldn't summon the energy.

I was no longer hopeless, though; in fact I was longing for the future to arrive, a future beyond England. But for now, I had to find ways of occupying the present. Without a dog to walk, I sought to distract myself from missing her by taking up running. There was a footpath that formed a circuit – beside the river, then across fields and back to the centre of the market town – that was just the right length for a beginner to manage. Slowly, my energy levels started to increase. I also stopped drinking, fed up with the tutting disapproval of every health professional. I was finally persuaded that drinking was interfering with the efficacy of the medication, and I hoped that my sleep might also improve. I wanted to be well and I wanted to be able to sleep so I thought it was worth a try. One day when there was no wine left in the house that was it.

Strangely, I didn't crave chardonnay the way I expected I would, having been on intimate terms with it for so long. If it wasn't in the fridge, I didn't look for it. If I could resist the wine section at the supermarket, distracting myself with the cake section instead, I would be fine at home without it. But if I had secretly hoped that quitting drinking would help reduce my weight I was disappointed: substituting cake for chardonnay simply maintained the status quo.

I wouldn't describe myself as happy but I was beginning to be a little more interested in the world again. I knew I was still fragile. I had bad days where I couldn't get out of bed, dozing through the morning to make up for missed sleep overnight. I went through the motions at work. Going out into the world was still mostly scary. But there were chinks in the darkness, moments of calm or delight, like getting out of my car after a 12-hour day of teaching and meetings one autumn evening to see the harvest moon rising above the lightly blown mist moving through the river reeds.

The next day, as I was tidying the kitchen before leaving late for work, there was a knock on the door. I opened it to find two neatly dressed men. One smiled and said, *We are going around asking the neighbours this question: Will suffering ever end?* With this, he produced a pamphlet from his briefcase, fittingly titled *Will Suffering Ever End?*

No, thank you, I said, and shut the door.

What a stupid thing to say. What did I mean? *No, suffering will never end?* Or *no, thank you, I don't want it to ever end?* Did I believe that suffering was inescapable? Or was I so habituated to a depressed state of mind that its removal would be even more unsettling?

I knew the smiling man thought he already had the answer to his question because I knew that particular story well. I had been taught it from earliest childhood as a star pupil at Sunday school. Yes, suffering would end with death, but (he thought) for the lucky few, death would mark the beginning of a new life of endless contentment.

As I returned to wiping down the kitchen bench-tops, instead of my usual angry response to such intrusions and the peddling of simplistic solutions, I wondered what the neighbours were saying. *We are going around asking the neighbours this question*, the smiling man had said. What was the word on the street about suffering?

The Journeyman had given me a workbook on mindfulness, a large-format, bullet-pointed, step-by-step guide that had its own solution to suffering. *If you've ever been deeply unhappy with your life for any length of time*, it began, *you know how difficult it can be to do anything about it.*

It was possibly the least inspiring book I have ever encountered. It made mindlessness seem like a more appealing option.

And I hate raisins, so that much-lauded mindfulness exercise that involves eating a single raisin for several minutes was a further deterrent.

When I had tried to explain to the Journeyman how unhelpful and patronising I found *Mindfulness for Morons* and its *programme designed specifically to help you deal with persistent unwanted mood states*, he dismissed my response as resistance and outlined the empirical evidence for the success of mindfulness techniques in people with symptoms like mine. If I applied myself and completed the homework, he insisted, in eight weeks I could learn new skills to empower myself.

We had a long discussion about the difference between things that are *simple* (authentic, humble, rustic) and things that are *simplistic* (reductive, facile, superficial). Basically, he thought both were the same thing. He also thought my fondness for nuance and ambiguity was part of my problem.

He was probably right (not about simplistic being a good thing; it's not, okay?). It was a lost cause. My immersion in literature had convinced me that a sensitivity to nuance, like a capacity for strong feeling, enriched our lives. I wanted mindfulness to be like *hearing the grass grow and the squirrel's heart beat*, as George Eliot put it: an intensity of perception and attention that is almost too much to bear but that reassures you that you are fully alive. Instead, I was presented with a manual of instructions that promised to give me back control of my attention, a kind of steady hand on the tiller of the psyche so that I could stay on course and arrive, unruffled, in the safe harbour of mental health.

No matter how ill and miserable my disorder had made me, I did not want to be someone who followed an *itinerary for each day's journey, spelled out in detail*, as *Mindfulness for Morons* offered. I wanted to be one of those people Virginia Woolf described, for whom *any turn in the wheel of sensation has the power to crystallise and transfix the moment upon which its gloom or radiance rests.*

In *Middlemarch,* George Eliot wrote that the reason we don't hear the squirrel's heart beat is because *the quickest of us walk about well wadded with stupidity.* I was as well wadded as the next person but my perception of everyday life was currently calibrated at a level that made me feel I could practically hear bacteria growing. Such (imaginary) sensitivity had not, however, led me to the kind of altruistic connection with others that Eliot espoused. I was no Dorothea Brooke; for starters, I could never visit the sick. I was forced to concede that the insistence of authors I loved – on the idea that an acute level of perception was life-enhancing – offered no practical solution to managing a phobic sense of siege from contact with the everyday world.

Soon after I parted ways with the Journeyman, however, I read Marion Milner's *A Life of One's Own,* in which she discovers what would now be called mindfulness – a term she never uses. Seeking to regain pleasure and meaning through closer observation of the stuff of everyday life, Milner describes how she stumbled on a state of heightened awareness that helped sustain her through the challenges of marriage, motherhood and her early career in the 1920s, before she became a leading figure in the Middle Group of the British Psychoanalytic Society. She talks about how, while she was performing some ordinary activities that engaged her mind (and hands) at one level, she began to experience a state of mind that combined contentment with a new ability to gain a wider perspective on her life.

Milner makes clear that this development was not about reconciling herself to a prescribed feminine role; what interested her was how to be a feeling, thinking body, able to respond fully to the variety of life's experiences. Milner called this state of mind *detachment,* but what she described did not seem so much a transcendence of the material realm, nor a lack of attachment to her daily life, more an intensity of attention that engaged both body and mind:

> This spreading of some vital essence of myself was a new gesture, more diffuse than the placing of awareness beyond myself which I had tried with music; it was more like a spreading of invisible sentient

feelers, as a sea anemone spreads wide its feathery fingers. Also I saw now that my usual attitude to the world was a contracted one, like the sea anemone when disturbed by a rough touch, like an amoeba shut within protective walls of its own making.

And what was Milner doing when she experienced this epiphany? Darning stockings. She had previously derived no enjoyment from sewing – *I was usually clumsy-fingered, fumbling and impatient to be finished,* she writes – but in this state she experienced both *a sense of ease* and improved competence that in turn gave her pleasure in this routine task.

From this discovery while darning stockings, Milner records how she extrapolated to a more general *gesture* or disposition, *simply to press my awareness out against the limits of my body till there was vitality in all my limbs and I felt smooth and rounded.* In this state, she also noted a change in her breathing that corresponds to what we might describe as a form of meditation. Everyday actions like sewing, then, became the means by which Milner learnt a new way to inhabit her body and escape the treadmill of thoughts that drained life of pleasurable moments. The work of her hands led her to a changed state of both mind and body – a spreading and interconnected realm of enhanced sensation and attention, despite the ordinary setting in which it occurred.

🌱

I've never darned a stocking. In fact, I can't sew at all, but I can knit. I am such a non-sewer that I gave up knitting items of clothing, as eventually the knitted pieces needed to be sewn together and I always ended up with puckered seams of lumpy, clumsily sewn stitches and, as a result, shapeless, ill-fitting sweaters or cardigans.

My failure at sewing is despite the fact that, as a feminine-gendered product of the Australian education system, I was taught sewing every week from the ages of six to 14, most memorably by the terrifying Mrs Stone in late primary school. She could subdue the most recalcitrant girls with her Medusa stare and, at least once every lesson, would explode with rage at the pathetic handiwork of some unfortunate girl who approached her seeking help with wayward seams. I was a poor student in her class and lived in fear of provoking such tirades. My normal compliance – and success – in the rest of my schooling had no effect on Mrs Stone; she recognised only my manifold failings as a seamstress and took them as a personal affront. Her constant ill-temper reinforced my sense that domestic occupations were provoking and made one unhappy; my mother, who kept a pristine house, was never happy in her housekeeping.

To make matters worse, these weekly sewing lessons took place in the primary-school library, our desks in close proximity to the shelves that beckoned me, siren-like, with the enchantment of their titles or spine designs; I often gave in to temptation, sneaking a book off the shelf and onto my lap where I hoped it would be out of sight of the beady-eyed Mrs Stone. Woe betide if she caught you reading instead of concentrating your attention on sewing elastic into your lemon-yellow seersucker bloomers. (I had no clue what bloomers were, incidentally, nor did Mrs Stone enlighten us when we began our term-long project, so imagine my surprise at the end of term to discover that I had made a pair of puffy knickers, more like an Elizabethan gentleman's slops than any underwear known to girls in the 1970s.) To this day, the sight – or, worse, the touch – of a seersucker tablecloth gives me a momentary chill.

Unlike sewing, however, knitting was one of the few domestic skills I acquired in childhood. I was taught by my mother and my grandmother, both highly skilled knitters who patiently corrected my early failures and were always able to find a lost stitch and restore it to its rightful place. As long as my mother was willing to sew up the seams, add buttons if required and press the cardigan into shape, I was able to pass as a reasonable knitter.

During that autumn and early winter while I first lived alone in England, I knitted constantly, making three throw rugs in quick succession, often with one over my lap while engaged in knitting the next. I can't say I experienced the *spreading of invisible sentient feelers* that Milner described in *A Life of One's Own*, but knitting calmed me, reconciled me to inhabiting the present moment, and reassured me that my body was not simply a collection of debilitating symptoms but had some creative capacity, even when I couldn't write.

Each of these throw rugs, however, had glaring errors in the simple lace pattern. Usually, such mistakes would bother me so much that I would have to unpick and correct them before proceeding, but I decided to live with them, to accept the fact – every time I looked at them – that imperfection is a part of daily life. The rugs still kept me warm. They still felt soft to the touch.

Quilters talk about the Amish tradition of the 'humility block' in quilting: one square of the quilt has a deliberate error, intended to remind the devout quilter that only God is perfect. Apparently this humility block tradition is just a myth, but it is endlessly recycled on quilting websites and in books about quilting, raising the question as to why it is perpetuated. It could be that quilting is such a painstaking task that mistakes invariably occur and quilters like the reassurance of the humility block. Or it could be that the myth meets a need – to accept our imperfections, however these are justified, whatever our state of grace. I know that on days when I was feeling low the sight of my knitting errors made me feel worse, but on better days I focused on the pleasure of the process rather than the perfection of the outcome.

If quilters like their 'traditions', knitters seem to be fascinated by famous knitters. Go to any knitting blog and you may be surprised to see how often Virginia Woolf is mentioned. The wonderful portrait of Virginia knitting (or crocheting? it's a subject of some debate) painted by her sister Vanessa Bell receives much comment as a kind of celebrity endorsement of knitting, but even more significant for bloggers is Virginia's statement (in a letter to Leonard Woolf in March 1912, around the same time as Vanessa's portrait) that *Knitting is the saving of life*. Unfortunately, most bloggers cannot resist the rather crass conclusion that *knitting only saved her temporarily*, as one puts it, before continuing:

> it's comforting to think of knitting as the therapy that helped stave off her suicide for some 30+ years ... allowing her the time to write her masterpieces.

So no knitting, no *Mrs Dalloway*, it seems.

In her letter, though, Virginia described her knitting as part of a gradual return to mental health, intended to reassure Leonard of her recovery – *I now feel very clear, calm, and move slowly* – but there is also a playful tone of self-mockery as she talks about how her brother Adrian had taken up knitting too and how it had transformed the lively, chatty siblings into quieter, contemplative souls. Knitting can't save your life, but it can change the way you feel.

I like to think of knitting as a kind of fretwork, a practice that creates decorative patterns of intersecting lines – similar to the ornamental architectural features in wood or stone usually termed fretwork, but in yarn – that allows one simultaneously to work on a vexed or troubled mind, soothing whatever one is fretting about. A less common meaning of fret is a *slow and gradual destructive action, such as caused by rust or disease or friction,* and that seems to me a fitting analogy for the process by which dark or anxious thoughts wear away at our resilience, our capacity for pleasure or meaningful activity. For me, then, fretwork is anything that allows us to work at stopping or reversing that corrosion, especially processes that direct our attention to our hands and away from our troubled mind. Connecting and interweaving threads or fibres, as in knitting or weaving, says something about a capacity to link or bind things together, taking a single thread and, over time, producing a durable, protective or ornamental object.

Knitting is comprised of stitches and holes: you make a gap and then you close it up, creating intervals that look like a mess in process but come together to form a pattern. It is a continuous process of doing and undoing, going forwards and backwards along rows, casting on and casting off. Each stitch is tiny; the process by which the hands guide the needles and hold the yarn is repetitive and a child can do it. But something appears out of almost nothing, simply a strand of yarn around a pair of needles. Over and over again.

Give me a knitting pattern rather than a mindfulness workbook any day.

9.

How
alive
am I
willing
to be?

In her wonderful book on writing, *Bird by Bird*, Anne Lamott offers the brutal advice: *Write as if your parents are dead*, because they are probably the ones who told you not to write in the first place.

It's true, they did. I learned as a teenager that I could be punished for writing and that words could be dangerous. As an avid reader throughout childhood, and like many bookworms, I had assumed a natural affinity with writing. One day I would be a writer, I thought, with little idea of what that would entail. But I had suddenly stopped writing at 13 when I arrived home from school one day to find my mother waiting for me as I came through the front door.

Never a good sign.

She instantly launched into a tirade about my disobedient behaviour. Despite clear parental prohibition, I had, she charged, *been leaving the high-school hall during the socials* – the quaint name for the school dances held at my country high school in the early 1970s – *and, even worse* – far, far worse – *kissing boys*.

There was only one way she could have discovered this information between the time I left for school in the morning and the time I returned home that afternoon: she must have found and read my diary, despite its clear instruction on the first page: *No reading beyond this point.* I remember the cold fury I felt, a chilling hardness that left no room for fear of punishment because I knew my anger was justified. The enormity of what she had done far outweighed my minor infraction, a few weeks back, of leaving a suffocatingly hot hall, full of sweaty and exuberant teenagers, every one of whom also left during the band breaks, to sit in the cool night air in the adjoining grandstand or on the benches by the sports field under the watchful eye of teachers armed with torches.

I had made no real attempt to hide my diary beyond keeping it in my desk, so confident was I that my privacy would be respected. Now, I cannot recall how I had come to have this simple trust, because that afternoon marked a point-of-no-return in my relationship with my mother that has blotted out much of whatever might have existed before.

And, yes, I had described in my diary the tentative kisses with my first high-school boyfriend sitting in the grandstand (a crush of such innocent inexperience on both sides that we practically ignored each other during the regular school day and it all fizzled out in a matter of weeks).

My mother said, *I have no choice but to punish you for your disobedience.*

Even though you had no right to read that? I challenged.

Yes, she said. *And I will tell your father when he gets home and we will decide on your punishment.*

While we waited for my father's return, however, and as my mother's initial anger cooled, she became increasingly upset in the face of my unyielding coldness. I retreated to my room but she followed me there, weeping and distraught, asking me for forgiveness, saying she would never do it again. I was appalled at her display. I wanted it to stop. I wanted her to leave my room. *I* should be the one crying. But she kept crying, kept saying, *I'm sorry, I'm so sorry.* Faced with her emotional display, my only option was to detach, deceive, refuse to succumb. The only way she would leave, I realised, was if I said,

Okay, it's all right. So I did, but I was lying. It wasn't all right. And I felt contempt for her, needing the forgiveness of the powerless one. She had willingly surrendered her power to me and it was a valuable lesson, despite the humiliation of exposure that I felt. I never wanted to be made to feel weak and exposed in that way again.

By the time my father came home the *Sturm und Drang* was over. My parents discussed my crimes in private before communicating my sentence to me: I was grounded for two weeks and banned from attending the next social. I never felt close to my mother again after that day.

But more had changed that day than just my relationship with my mother. She had taken something innocent and twisted it into something dirty. She had read my words as if they were shameful; she had used my words against me.

So I abandoned my diary. Writing betrayed you, shamed you. People discovered bad things about you in your writing. They saw you were a bad person, a person of bad thoughts and bad deeds.

I still hate people reading over my shoulder, even if it is just a newspaper. It feels invasive and somehow makes me feel culpable. If my husband, entering a room to find me with a book in hand, asks, *What are you reading?* I always feel a momentary fizz of anger. *Don't ask me that, it's none of your business* is the reflex response I feel but never say, as if the question itself is some kind of violation. Instead I pause, take a breath, and try to make my voice sound like a normal person's before I reply.

When you consider how much of my life I have spent reading books – given my career – it is laughable, if not downright odd, that I feel so uncomfortable to disclose what I am reading. For many years I imagined everyone shared my irritation at being questioned in this way, as if it were poor etiquette, akin to enquiring about someone's excretory practices. What I am reading is a deeply personal thing, not for your approval or appraisal; it crosses some kind of boundary for me between book/self and world. It is as if I am thinking, *Let me keep this to myself, let me have this, without your prying or judgement or criticism.*

Growing up, everything I read, watched or listened to was closely scrutinised by my fundamentalist parents and my choices often earned their disapproval in ways that confused me. Despite their dogmatic beliefs, my parents loved music and movies of many kinds. My mother took me to see *Help!* at the cinema when I was small, such was her love of the Beatles (although she later gave away her complete Beatles LP collection in a fit of conscience). My father talked endlessly about his favourite Hollywood films of the 1940s and 1950s. When I asked childish questions about lyrics or plot lines that I couldn't figure out, however, a studied parental reticence often prevailed. (My mother, for instance, refused to explain to me what happened in *Camelot*, one of her favourite musicals that she regularly sang along to while the record played, because it would have meant disclosing that the plot centred on adultery.) I was rebuked when I sang lyrics I was too young to understand had a sexual meaning – even though I had only learned them because they played repeatedly on our hi-fi.

So the power of words to corrupt you – unknowingly – meant that, somehow, you could become complicit in something questionable just through reading or repeating the words of others. Writing your own words, it seemed, was even more fraught. If I ever felt drawn to writing, there was always something that pulled me back, made me wary of committing myself to paper for all to see.

In the midst of this breakdown, however, even while I felt myself withdrawing from life and hope and meaning, I turned back to writing as if my life depended on it.

Looking back at how she had started to write, Virginia Woolf explained how exceptional moments, moments charged with either positive or negative feeling that created a powerful impression akin to a shock, evoked in her such a strong desire to explain what had happened, to understand what had triggered that response, that she had to write them down. *I feel*, Woolf wrote,

> that I have had a blow; but it is not, as I thought as a child, simply a blow from an enemy hidden behind the cotton wool of daily life; it is or will become a revelation of some order; it is a token of some real thing behind appearances; and I make it real by putting it into words. It is only by putting it into words that I make it whole; this wholeness means that it has lost its power to hurt me; it gives me, perhaps because by doing so I take away the pain, a great delight to put the

severed parts together. Perhaps this is the strongest pleasure known to
me … From this I reach what I might call a philosophy; at any rate
it is a constant idea of mine; that behind the cotton wool is hidden a
pattern … And this conception affects me every day. I prove this, now,
by spending the morning writing … I feel that by writing I am doing
what is far more necessary than anything else.

For Woolf, writing takes away the power to be hurt or to suffer
pain and instead brings a reintegration or reconnection of what had
been violently ruptured. Woolf is, of course, not the only writer
to see writing as a means of imposing order and meaning on what
might otherwise be inchoate or traumatic experience, and thus to
find, through writing, a pattern that explains, comforts or repairs.
But through her account of exceptional moments turned into words,
of how a *blow* can become a *revelation* that helps puts things back
together, I came to understand how important it was to explore pain
through words.

By writing I am doing what is far more necessary than anything else.

The more I wrote, however, the more things seemed to come apart
rather than come back together. For me, writing didn't offer revelation
or wholeness so much as, in the midst of symptoms that robbed me
of my sense of self, another form of *dis*-assembling my feelings, my
thoughts, my memories. Somehow, though, writing also helped me to
feel alive again. It lifted the cotton wool to uncover, if not a pattern of
soothing reassurance, something that felt pulsing and raw beneath.

Anne Lamott talks about the trust and the courage, as well as
the elation, of writing, because *being a writer is ultimately about asking
yourself, How alive am I willing to be?* I knew now that I wanted to be
alive, but *how* alive?

10.

A
garden
in the
antipodes

After a long, mild English autumn, winter had arrived suddenly with gale-force winds and lashing rain, and I was grateful to be working from home. No run today.

There had been a ladybird in my cottage for a couple of days. I had first seen the tiny creature in the kitchen, walking along the edge of the empty dishrack. Later I spied her on the handle of the kettle and moved her to the thick, waxy leaves of the money plant on the windowsill. When I returned to the kitchen in the early hours of the morning for a glass of water she was still there, busy among the leaves.

I was shortly to fly away home to a place I had never been before. In a reversal of the process by which Europeans in New Zealand continued to refer to Britain as *home* well into the twentieth century, even though many had never set foot there, I felt that my home was a place that I had only seen in pictures so far. It was on a ridge above Matakana, a village I had visited briefly once before. On that occasion, walking down the steps to the riverside marketplace, I had unaccountably welled up, overcome by an intense feeling that this was where I wanted to be, where I should be. I had been on a short trip back to New Zealand for a conference, after which I had reluctantly returned to England, little imagining that just over a year later we would buy a house there. Now, Matakana was still not-yet-home: I was coming back to New Zealand for a period of study leave, but I was committed to returning to England for the summer term that started in May in order to complete the duties of the northern academic year.

The flight took more than a day, from northern winter to southern summer, followed by a two-hour drive from the airport to our house. Crossing Auckland harbour and the endless suburbs, then past farmland and forests thick with giant tree-ferns, we eventually reached Matakana. The main road through the village soon turned into a steep and winding ascent before we turned off onto a gravel road that led to our house on the ridge, perched on a few hectares of paddocks and covenanted bush overlooking the Hauraki Gulf.

The view was arresting. I got out of the car and stood, for some minutes, taking in the sweep of the hills to the ocean and islands, various shades of hazy blue in the distance. When I made it inside, I walked straight through to the verandah that ran the length of the house, pulled back by the sight of the distant sea, by the mānuka trees framing the paddocks, by the tūī feeding on nectar in the flax that surrounded our house. Within the first hour, I heard the silvery trill of my favourite bird, the riroriro, the grey warbler, hidden out of sight in the bush.

For the first couple of days, however, I felt strangely numb and disoriented. All my familiar routines of Kentish life – the morning run, daily writing, solitary meals, knitting in the evening – were disrupted by a return to the family home in a new location and a new season, summer replacing winter. Obsessive-compulsives rely on daily routines for a sense of calm and control, so I was thrown by the strangeness of it all. I felt a slight resurgence of my depression and, for the first time since starting medication six months ago, I forgot to take my pills for two days.

I had to re-learn how to talk to my husband and son after four months apart, how to live with other people. The first day I was unusually quiet, not able to verbalise the flood of impressions and sensations that I felt.

Is this OK? Do you like it here? Did we do the right thing buying this place? my husband asked.

Yes, yes, definitely, I said, but it didn't seem real yet.

In his first weeks back in New Zealand we had phoned and Skyped most days. The 12-hour time difference meant that one of us was starting a day as the other was finishing it. We talked through the virtues and pitfalls of buying a house this far from the city, weighing up the relative merits of the lifestyle and the lower property prices against the distance to work and school, the improvements that the house and land would need, the lack of conveniences that city dwellers took for granted (like mains water supply). Now I saw for myself what he had seen then: an unremarkable and rather boxy 20-year-old timber house among gently sloping paddocks surrounded by trees, with the blue horizon and big skies encompassing all. It was perfect.

ᴡ

The first morning I woke up in our new house, I drank coffee in bed watching the sun rise over the ocean, while a tūī worked its way from flower to flower on the flax outside my window. In the farthest paddock, Australian magpies warbled and Australian rosellas squawked as they skimmed low before landing in the long grass to feast on the abundant seed. I seemed to be in a place that fused all the antipodean landscapes that I loved – bush, birds and ocean – so that it seemed familiar and new at the same time.

Within two days, the angry skin rash that had inexplicably broken out all around my neck a month before – *I'm allergic to England,* I had joked to my osteopath – had disappeared. I started to relax.

My morning routine changed. Instead of a solitary run along the flats of the River Stour, I now ran the length of a white-sand beach framed between two headlands while my husband had an early swim. Sometimes the dog came too, but she would always succumb to the irresistible distraction of rabbits hidden up in the sand dunes and disappear from sight. I would slow to a walk, calling her, then stop altogether, debating whether to seek her out or wait for her to reappear above the grassy dune, to look down on me with ears cocked and tongue lolling before bounding down the slope to rejoin me.

It was the start of the Christmas break so the whole family was in holiday mode. My daughter and her partner flew up from the South Island. During the day we visited beaches, played cards, went out for ice-cream or coffee, or simply sat on the verandah looking out to sea. I read voraciously – fiction, memoirs, essays, philosophy, poetry – and, for the first two weeks, I napped during the day and slept at night in a way I had forgotten was possible.

With almost daily swimming, my frozen shoulder began to free up. Months of treatment in England had brought no relief from the pain and I had limited movement in my left arm. My osteopath was bewildered by the lack of any improvement. On my first swim at Ōmaha Beach, I thoughtlessly tried to dive under an approaching wave and cried out with the pain. I found I could only dog paddle, unable to raise my arm above my head. Within two weeks, however, I could move my arm in a wide arc and, by midsummer, was swimming freely. The pain had gone. If England had given me the cold shoulder, New Zealand was thawing me out.

In those first weeks, though, I couldn't write. I could only store up impressions of sky, bush and sea, of the silver-grey lichen that grew in small tufts on tree trunks and fence posts alike, of the new furry brown fronds of ponga uncurling a little further each day throughout the garden and bush. There was so much to notice, so much to absorb. I didn't yet know the names of all the North Island trees and plants that surrounded me, the *green-blue, / green-blue / exhilaration of lively leafage on sky-spaces,* as poet Ursula Bethell puts it.

Born in Surrey in 1874, Bethell is best known for her poems about her Christchurch garden, but in fact she moved back and forth between England and New Zealand for much of her life, an unsettled settler like me. In a letter written towards the end of her life that echoed the botanical imagery of her poems, she warned a friend that he should not see her as typically English:

75

I wouldn't be a good specimen – I am too variegated … That's one of the sad things about me! – I don't belong anywhere in particular – I've dodged to and fro – … I'm not a fair sample – I have not been able to settle …

Bethell did not begin writing poetry until she was almost 50 (another fact that endears her to me), after she had moved to the house where she established her garden. Her first collection, *From a Garden in the Antipodes*, was published in 1929 under the pseudonym Evelyn Hayes and was described on the dust jacket as

Episodes in verse from
a *New Zealand* garden
introducing
the *Gardener,*
the *Housewife,*
a distant *Friend,*
a large *Persian Cat,*
a small *Japanese Orange-Tree*
Plants, Pests, Postmen
and Passers-by.

Who wouldn't want to read a collection like that? (The orange tree even has a name: *O little Omi-Kin-Kan.*)

From a Garden in the Antipodes is grounded in the events of everyday life. Peeling potatoes, pulling weeds or watering the garden are all subjects worthy of poetry for Bethell, as in the opening lines of 'Incident':

Today I woke at half past five and roused
My so reluctant frame, and went to hose
Thirsty hydrangeas and my parched green peas.

Sometimes Bethell's poetry feels dated or over-fussy, but much of this collection is written *in plain words* as its opening poem puts it. What more need be said about a hard day's labour in the garden than *Muddy boots. Scratched hands. Deep sleep?* Out of such incidents and images, a life is made. There are grumpy poems about the drudgeries of housework and gardening (*I find vegetables fatiguing / And would rather buy them in a shop*); short, spare poems devoted to supposedly uninspiring subjects like her garage, *a structure of excessive plainness*; and self-deprecating poems where she mocks her own aesthetic pretensions to genteel gardening:

> I said: I will go into the garden and consider roses;
> I will observe the deployment of their petals,
> And compare one variety with another.
> But I was made to sit down and scrape potatoes.

The implied voice of practicality and potatoes here, Bethell's partner Effie Pollen (the *Housewife*), is a presence throughout this collection. There can't be too many poems devoted to a couple's domestic disagreements over their respective domains – house and garden – as in 'Controversy':

> There is perpetual contention
> Between the guardians of the dwelling house and the
> demesne.
>
> Shall the garden be a paradise,
> And the inside of the cottage a shambles?
>
> Or contrariwise, the garden a wilderness,
> While we preserve the image of a Dutch interior?

These are still good questions. My husband is a devoted gardener who thinks it is more important to mow the grass than change the bed linen when house guests are expected. I would rather admire the garden than weed it. But we both peel potatoes (on alternate evenings). I think that Jenny Bornholdt, another gardening poet, has it right when she says *the garden / is as much poem as this poem is. And the washing and the coffee / are also poem.*

11.

Much
to
unravel

W hen the English nature writer Richard Mabey moved from
the Chilterns to East Anglia (not a big move for those accustomed
to antipodean distances), it triggered a series of existential questions
for him: *Where do I belong? What's my role? How, in social, emotional,
ecological terms, do I find a way of fitting?* As he goes on to describe in
Nature Cure, Mabey's move was also part of a journey back to mental
health. For me, too, returning to health involved questions about
where I belonged: not just where I wanted to *be* – I knew that, I
wanted to be in New Zealand – but what I wanted to *do*. My career
was in England; there was no prospect of a similar position on either
island of New Zealand. So far, then, my letter of resignation remained
unwritten.

During one of my sessions with the Journeyman in which we had
talked about my desire to return to New Zealand, he asked, *What will
happen when you are back there?* I had shrugged. It seemed too obvious.
I will be there, I said. *I will be. There.*

I couldn't see past the simple fact of returning. I saw images – green valleys, beaches, bushland – that implied a still point of observation by some new, calm self. That seemed enough. But now that I was home, I saw what he had been trying to nudge me towards: was that really enough?

In England, immersed in a homesickness for New Zealand that embarrassed me with its intensity, I was only aware of an urgent desire for home. *I'm homesick* offered a kind of shorthand term I could use to explain my low mood to colleagues when I had a few teary moments at the office in the first months, but it also seemed such an anachronistic condition to own up to in a twenty-first century globalised world of speedy mobility, mass migration and instant communication. To be homesick implied a temporary state that could be overcome in time, as I settled in. Nobody expects homesickness to be permanent.

I wasn't sure, though, whether I was entitled to such a strong feeling; my emotional response to New Zealand was not grounded in any historical connection or claim. I was not born there, I had only lived there for eight years, but somehow New Zealand had supplanted the Australian coastal landscape of my childhood as the place where I felt I belonged. But what could tūrangawaewae mean for me, just another unsettled settler, displaced by choice? Was I permitted to claim this term to explain my desire to feel grounded, connected and empowered in Aotearoa? I was well aware that, in postcolonial New Zealand, the concept of belonging is historically fraught and impinges on everyone, Māori and Pākehā, in diverse, complex and often painful ways.

When I moved to England I had discovered one positive aspect of *not* belonging: I did not feel implicated; I had nothing at stake in its history, at least nothing for which I felt culpable. As a white Australian living in Australia, it had never been possible to shake a sense of shame at one's own complicity with colonial dispossession. What had never been properly acknowledged or compensated at a national level can't be brushed aside by individual citizens. We had all benefited – and continued to benefit – from invasion and genocide. Our homes occupied land that belonged to someone else. The river swimming place that I had loved as a child was next to a beautiful island from which the Gumbaynggirr people had been summarily displaced so that the white community could turn it into a golf course in the 1960s. Both my parents regularly played on that course. Once, early one morning before school, my father took me to the island while the low river mist was still on the fairways, to show me a plover's nest with three speckled eggs on open ground near one of the putting greens.

In England, although I was technically classed as an immigrant, I had in another sense *gone back to where I came from*, in that familiar chant that, paradoxically, unites anti-immigrant and radical indigenous campaigners alike. My mother's parents had emigrated to Sydney from East Sussex in the 1920s; my father's family background – or his name at least – traced back to Yorkshire roots. I was a part of the empire striking back and was often bemused to find that my colonial background provoked responses from the mildly patronising to the unwittingly insulting (such as when interlocutors, knowing I had moved from New Zealand, assumed I was a Kiwi and took the opportunity to observe *at least you're not an Australian*, or words to that effect). So in England I felt as if I was off the hook. I may not have fitted in but at least I was not haunted by the thought I was occupying land to which I had no legitimate claim. My ancestors had lived in the next county so, I reasoned, I had some entitlement to be in this part of the world.

At first, I had tried to foster a sense of my roots in southeast England, to identify with the landscape in which I found myself, beginning with our garden. The garden of England. In the early spring, crocuses, snowdrops and daffodils appeared, then the blush-pink magnolia tree bloomed, to be followed later by tulips and peonies. Spring also brought the apple, pear, plum and apricot trees into blossom, followed in due course by their abundant fruit, as well as nuts from the Kentish cob nut tree (if the dog didn't crunch them up, shell and all, first). A previous owner had planted scores of rose bushes that bloomed all summer long in large garden beds and climbed on frames and fences. As the summer continued, the purple buddleia would be alive with butterflies: rusty-red peacocks with arresting large blue and yellow 'eyes' ringed in black on their wings, yellow Brimstones, Red Admirals and, occasionally, the ragged-

winged Commas. On bad days I liked to stand under the buddleia
in the corner of the garden with the afternoon sun full on my back,
breathing in the heady, honey fragrance and watching the butterflies.
The silence of the butterflies in their jerky flight from bloom to
bloom offered a respite from the black noise in my head, and the
summer warmth triggered a body memory of other places where the
sun was a more regular presence.

When we had initially viewed this garden in the depths of winter,
just a few days after arriving in England, the flower beds were bare,
the roses merely pruned sticks, allowing the trees to dominate. The
two tallest trees, an oak and an Australian eucalyptus, stood facing each
other on opposite sides at the back of the house. We took it as a good
omen that we could just as harmoniously blend the old and the new,
our past with our present, and make a home here. (When we sold
the thatched house, the new English owners cut down the gum tree
within weeks of taking possession.)

In Dunedin, with a climate not dissimilar to England (except that
Kentish summers were warmer!), gardens are commonly modelled on
English counterparts, with bulbs and roses, rhododendrons and copper
beeches. Moving to Dunedin from Perth, an arid city on the edge of
the desert where the soil was little more than sand, it was a delight to
see the abundance of European flowers and foliage that thrived in our
Otago garden. But at our new home in Matakana, the garden – still a
work in progress – is almost entirely green and mostly native, full of
lush ferns, trees and clumps of flax, with its shiny, sword-shaped leaves
that grow up to three metres and rustle audibly in the lightest breeze.
The garden blends seamlessly with our stand of covenanted bush,
where there are tree ferns like ponga and whekī, clusters of mānuka,
and the larger trees – rimu, tōtara, kahikatea. So many shades of green
and textures of foliage rivalling for the eye's attention with the blues
of the more distant sea view. Next summer, we hope the pōhutukawa
we have planted will bloom.

My husband is beginning to clear a narrow, simple path through
the thickest part of the bush, careful to disturb as little as possible of
the luxuriant growth. We want to be able to feel fully immersed in its
green world, where it is cool on the hottest days and protected from
any winds that blow along the ridge. Standing on this path, the micro-

world of ferns, epiphytes and lichens comes into focus. On a small
tree by the path's entrance, a patch of black lichen growing at eye-
level would not look out of place adorning the lapel of a dandy from
the decadent 1890s. It is green–black, the thallus like a large, flattened
carnation with the texture of the softest silk taffeta. Further in,
multiple mosses and miniature climbing ferns, a blend of viridescent
tints and patterns, interlace on the trunks of trees and saplings, from
roots to canopy. The smell of damp fertile earth envelops you and
the ground cushions your feet. It is softly yielding, neither muddy
nor entirely firm, a humus in which leaf matter is gradually breaking
down. The bracken ferns have browned but are still springy under
foot. A chair carried in here would subside softly into the earth as
you sat in it, perhaps even taking root as the moss and lichen began
their work, holding you in place as the chair sank imperceptibly
groundward. I want to sit there and be claimed, contained, by the
bush.

Writing in 1949, poet A.R.D. Fairburn, who, like Ursula Bethell,
had lived both in England and New Zealand, explored the desire to
withdraw from the world into nature. Fairburn's poem 'To a Friend
in the Wilderness' uses a dialogue form to consider both sides of the
question: faced with the evils of the modern world, should one retreat
to a simpler life of self-sufficiency in the nature of New Zealand?
    The friend in the wilderness urges:

> the sun is on the sea and the fish are biting,
> the garden is full, the fruit begins to fall.
> For God's sake chuck it, join me and share my crust,
> the world well lost. Make life a long week-end.

The pull of this request on the voice representing the poet is evident
as he recalls his friend's bush escape:

> In the crystal heat the cicadas
> crackle on sunlit walls, on pea-sticks dried and splintered,
> and among the macrocarpas:
> from thistle to cloudless blue the world is vibrant.

And the poet's desire to be settled, to be grounded in such a place, is strong:

> I have no wish to circle the globe,
> have no desire to travel
> beyond my chosen acre: would choose
> to live in peace in one place
> and make my life one stay:
> there is much to unravel, and much to piece together.

Reluctantly, though, the poet ultimately chooses the bonds of family, society and politics over those of male friendship and the bush:

> Old rebel, what is there left for me to say?
> … This is my world.
> These people are my clansmen, my accomplices.
> I share the crime. This guilt is my reprieve:
> I am alive, and I do not mean to leave
> till the game is up, and my hand has lost its power.
> These are my people.

Fairburn remained active in leftist politics and literature in New Zealand until his death in 1957, and while this poem reflects a strongly masculinist perspective of its time, it still speaks to me about the tension between finding a place in the world to belong and knowing what one's work in the world is, about the allure of escape and the complexity of belonging.

Does belonging derive from an acceptance of our place in the natural world? Or does it arise from doing, engaging and connecting with a wider social world beyond the self? If I wanted to retreat to nature, was that because it represented my best opportunity for healing, for refuge? Or was it simply a continuation of my desire to avoid contamination – part of my pathology, that is, not necessarily of my recovery? My longing to leave the dirt, noise and congestion of England behind and immerse myself in the natural environment of New Zealand was certainly a desire to escape contamination, but was it, could it be, more than that? Nature – at least, the transformed and domesticated nature that now surrounded me – could give me a safe space to heal and flourish, but when does comfort become a cocoon that signals a disavowal of messy, adult life? Was I just seeking to opt out of the chores of adulthood, of adulthood *as* chore, and return to an idealised version of my childhood, barefoot in the bush?

12.

Goats
in
fog

Although my pastoral fantasy of life in Kent had been such a disappointment, I still had high hopes for creating an antipodean idyll so, on an evening in late summer, our goats arrived on the Pet Courier bus. The three of them had travelled from Hawke's Bay in the company of a few dogs and a litter of tiny puppies destined for new homes in Northland. The puppies' mother, distraught at her separation from her litter who were in a basket on the front seat, barked aggressively in the cage next to the goats – but the goats were still reluctant to leave the van after their long day on the road. Eventually the driver managed to unload them and we led them to the lawn, where they pulled so hard at the grass with their teeth that – standing close to them – you could feel a vibration in the ground beneath you.

They were Rawhiti goats – a hardy, hybrid breed of small stature – and they had come from a dairy herd where each animal had been given a name. Myrtle and Marjoram were sisters, two of triplets born a year ago, while Pansy, the largest of the three, was a year older. I had wanted goats ever since I had visited a goat cheesemaker's farm outside Perth and been drawn in by the creatures' gentle but curious engagement with humans. Now I finally had enough space to adopt a few of my own.

It had been a day of drenching summer rain and as it was now dark we decided to keep the goats indoors for their first night, where they would be dry and safe. The laundry became a makeshift goat pen for the evening, but the small, unfamiliar space, following the stress of their trip, resulted in some aggressive head-butting by the two larger goats of the smallest, Myrtle, who took refuge in a corner. Fearing a tragedy on our first evening of goat custodianship, we separated them. Myrtle spent the night in the garage in the dog's old crate, where she seemed happy enough, allowing her nose to be stroked in between mouthfuls of hay.

In the morning we woke early to check on the goats and take them to their paddock. Pansy and Marjoram were reluctant to leave the laundry – now thoroughly imbued with *eau de chèvre* – but after some vigorous persuasion they followed us to the paddock, with a brief detour when they spied Myrtle in the garage and went to investigate. She was keen to come too and soon all three were in the paddock, where the grass was as tall as Myrtle. With plenty of space to share, there was none of the aggression of the previous night. Instead, the three kept close together, the younger ones following Pansy's lead as she gradually ventured a few steps further afield, and then a few more, all the time keeping a wary eye on us. After about 40 minutes, they had made their way to one corner of the field where a small tree provided a little shade and there they spent the morning, still with a weather eye on the creatures observing them from the verandah.

After only a few days, the goats started to run up to the gate when they spied me approaching with their buckets of fermented barley (only a cupful in each, but after the first day it became apparent that three goats meant three buckets to avoid too many horn incidents). Poor little Myrtle was usually shoved out of the way at the first opportunity by both Pansy and her own sister Marjoram, but she also took advantage of her smaller stature: so far, she was the only one who had managed an escape, wriggling under a gap in the fence into the paddock closest to the house.

After the barley is gone, I like to stay on with the goats for a while. The fur around their muzzles is incredibly soft, like velvet, although the rest of their coat is coarse and wiry, shading from dark brown to grey-brown (with the addition of distinctive white patches in the case of Pansy). They lick my fingers and then pucker their lips, revealing their small, even, harmless teeth. I feel no fear from their contact. I can't explain why. Rational explanation could never touch my phobias; now, the absence of contamination phobia is equally indecipherable.

While I am patting Pansy, the bossiest but the most eager for human contact, Marjoram suddenly lowers her head to the ground and, like a forklift, moves her head forward through the grass before raising it, her horns now festooned with flowering weeds, Ophelia-like. She walks off, unconcerned about the greenery she is wearing. I had not expected such insouciance to be so comforting, but there is a quality of acceptance that the goats somehow communicate to me in our daily encounters.

The goats rarely bleat and when they do they are like ventriloquists. Their mouths are closed and the sound seems to come from far away. Even standing close to them, it is difficult to believe that what sounds like distant bleating is in fact coming from a creature only an arm's length away. They are also discreet excreters, squatting almost demurely to pee, like a female cat or dog, and silently dropping small pellets of excrement in modest piles that are virtually invisible in the thick grass of the paddock.

I had a romantic whim that goats need bells. I also hoped that bells would help us to locate them if they found another way to escape the paddock (a persistent worry, given that thick bush bordered their field and they had quickly acquired a fondness for the leaves of a particular tree on the edge of the bush, which they strained to reach by standing on their hind legs against the boundary fence). One evening in the first week, my husband and I attempt to bell the goats. The goats are wise to our wish to catch them and trot off across the paddock, staying just out of reach, looking nervous, while we loiter ineffectually in a persistent drizzle. Eventually all three are belled but they are now skittish. For the next hour, we hear them trotting sporadically across the paddock in a vain attempt to outrun their bells, and I worry that

I have subjected these creatures to a damaging attempt at human mastery. Are goat bells unethical? And why had I not considered that question before I bought the bells?

Feminist philosopher Donna Haraway has proposed that we can learn how to relate to significant otherness, how to live well with others, through living alongside companion animals. The significant otherness of a dog, my doe-eyed whippet, had provided me with immense comfort during the depths of depression. When I could not accept myself, the dog was there, alongside me. She needed food, company and exercise but, beyond that, she made no demands on me, willing to cohabit with me in what felt like acceptance but was probably just a quiet coexistence. She was not-me, not-human; she was a dog, in all her doggy otherness. Both elegant and affectionate, she nonetheless had some revolting doggy habits that were a reminder that being domesticated was not the same as being refined or civilised (or any of those other terms that are just as dubious and value-laden when they are applied to some humans and not others). At a time when I couldn't enter public restrooms and marvelled at how I had ever been able to deal with babies' nappies on a regular basis, I would collect dog poop in a plastic bag without a second thought on our daily walks – such is the irrationality of phobias and the safe space that somehow my dog provided for me. As Haraway puts it, *Dogs are not surrogates for theory; they are not here just to think with. They are here to live with.*

Living with myself, with others, or with uncomfortable reality, has never come easily. 'Living with' – in the sense of tolerating, bearing with, or even thriving with – is a difficult undertaking when depression isolates me, casts me adrift from everything beyond the self. When I couldn't relate meaningfully to others, even my husband and children, the dog kept me connected to a world of living creatures, a place that was lighter and warmer than the just-me world of depression.

But what kind of relating could really exist between me and three goats? Could they be companion animals too? Were they just here for aesthetic or therapeutic purposes? Was this a justifiable reason for keeping animals? What did goats – intelligent as well as social creatures – want from me (apart from daily feeds of fermented barley)? What would living with goats entail? From the beginning, they seemed to regard me as more than simply an alien presence beyond the fence or an instrumentalist means to nutrition. A process of mutual adaptation seemed under way.

Despite the indignity of the bells, the goats settled in quickly and began to build what we fondly imagined to be affectionate bonds with their human caretakers. They trot to the closest fence whenever we arrive home, pushing their heads between the railings to come closer to us, regarding us intently and seeming to enjoy being patted, stroked or scratched. Sometimes, in their enthusiasm (or hunger), they jump up in the manner of a dog and put their front hooves on the chest of a bucket-bearing human. Oddly, they eschew kitchen scraps like lettuce leaves or pieces of apple, whereas a handful of cornflakes or a crust of bread is a treat for which the three of them compete. The sound of a goat crunching dry cornflakes is an unexpectedly pleasing one.

As the goats become more curious, however, they start to escape more frequently from the paddocks, whether in search of food or diversion. Their bells serve a useful purpose after all; when the tinkling is loud, I know the goats have found their way onto the back lawn or into a garden bed adjoining the house. One morning I find them grazing nonchalantly on the edge of the gravel driveway, the freedom of the open road just beyond as yet undiscovered. Another day I open the curtains of the living room to startle three goats standing on the verandah outside the glass doors, as if waiting to join us for breakfast. What started as the odd bit of chicken wire that my husband nailed to reinforce the fence at vulnerable points has gradually spread: there is now a stretch of continuous wiring below the lowest bar of the fence closest to the house (to the dog's dismay: the fence had until then provided two-way access – allowing her to squeeze under and chase the rabbits that peacefully share the paddocks with the goats).

One day, my husband discovers Pansy standing, Monarch-of-the-Glen style, on the roof of their shelter; a photo records this momentous occasion. If you want to know what a self-satisfied goat looks like, I can provide documentary evidence. It soon becomes evident, though, that this is not a one-off and in fact the shelter roof is a prized and hotly contested post. Only one goat can occupy it at a time, apparently, and as the largest and dominant goat it is usually Pansy, but sometimes it is Marjoram, and even Myrtle briefly appears there, before she is chased off the roof by one of the larger two, rebuking her insolence. The challenge for position on the roof is like a goatish version of Chicken: the first one there challenges the interloper, encouraging her towards the edge until she is forced to leap off into the grass a couple of metres below, surrendering her position to the victor.

The playful nature of the goats that emerges the more I watch them reminds me that the word *caper* derives from the Latin for goat. They do, indeed, caper about at times, especially in games of head-butting (surprisingly, often initiated by little Myrtle, even taking on Pansy, who good-naturedly joins in when she does not consider it beneath her dignity). One goat rears back on her hind legs, hanging in the air momentarily (think *Crouching Tiger, Hidden Dragon*), her head lowered, and, if her chosen sparring partner is willing, the two goats then butt each other, with the contact of their horns sounding like a light clash of sticks. Head-butting seems to carry a number of meanings, from playful capering to assertion of dominance (especially when food is involved), to something more like a form of contact between the creatures, a light touch of heads or horns like a reminder of relationship, or a renewal of goatly conversation after a long spell of solitary grazing and gazing in disparate parts of the paddocks.

Reflecting on the shelter-roof game, my husband decides to arrange some unused garden chairs and planks of wood in another part of the paddock as a kind of goat climbing-frame. He is concerned that they may become bored with just walking about in paddocks. The goats take to the climbing-frame immediately. With a single agile spring they can stand on the planks, but they also institute a variant of the roof game, in which only one may stand on the chairs/planks at a time, so they chase each other up and off the frame repeatedly, until one tires of it and wanders off to graze. Or they all decide to simply sit on the planks and sun themselves instead.

Later, when the wet winter arrives and the paddocks become increasingly muddy and even boggy in parts, the climbing-frame will serve another purpose: keeping their hooves dry. They will also acquire thicker winter coats, their goat hair softening and becoming more fleecy, protecting them effectively from the worst of the rain so that they are quite tolerant of standing out in showers; only downpours will see them retreat to their shelter. Marjoram's winter coat is particularly shaggy and much fairer than her summer fur; it looks uncannily like a 1980s spiral perm and is a bleached blonde colour, like Kylie in her *Neighbours* days. Luckily, she will become more inured to human contact (Marjoram, that is) as it is so satisfying to run your fingers through her soft woolly fleece, silky to the touch. When I feed them on cold mornings, holding a bucket while one or another goat leans against me as she eats, as they are each wont to do, I am surprised by how warm and dry they are, radiating heat that I can feel through my thick trousers as they munch through their food. They seem perfectly adapted both to their environment and to their proximity to humans – accepting the weather and our presence in their daily lives with equanimity.

But the winter is still months away, although the late summer weather is becoming increasingly unsettled, hot days alternating with spells of heavy, driving rain that bring a temporary coolness to our ridge. After one very wet night, the next morning the distant ocean is obscured by a thick mist. I chase the school bus all the way to Warkworth after my son and I watch it pull away from the only bus stop in the village just as we drive up. By the time I turn back into our driveway, it is pouring again and I am craving my deferred coffee and feeling a potentially housebound day stretch before me.

When the rain stops there is not a breath of wind, even along our usually breezy ridge, and the mist closes in and recedes repeatedly. The tall trees at the end of our paddocks are enveloped and then reappear. In the fog the goats' bells sound close, as if they are just outside this room, although they are all huddled in their shelter down in the paddock, sitting on the hay bales with their front legs folded beneath them. Their bells indicate when one shakes her head, stands to look out into the mist, or turns to scratch her flank with her horn. They seem to have infinite patience on days of bad weather, as they sit or stand quietly in their shelter, waiting for conditions to improve so they can return to grazing the paddocks. There seems no urgency in the life of a domestic goat. *She had all the composure of a goat* is not something you ever hear people say but I think it should be considered something of a compliment.

Goats are seriously under-represented in literature. If you take out the classical and biblical references, and those gruff billy goats, you aren't left with much, just the odd poem. The same goes for art. I have been a fan of Pre-Raphaelite art since I was an undergraduate, but William Holman Hunt's *The Scapegoat* is one of the ugliest paintings I have ever seen, with the doomed creature in a lurid, apocalyptic landscape gazing vacantly at the viewer. Hunt evokes no sympathy for the scapegoat, despite the fact that it is surrounded by the skeletal remains of its unfortunate predecessors. Its shaggy coat may be meticulously rendered in almost photographic detail but this scapegoat is weighed down by its symbolic value; we are given no sense of a living, breathing animal that we could smell or touch.

Sheep, on the other hand, have a long and illustrious cultural legacy. They may be synonymous with stupidity, but there are countless Romantic poems where *full-grown lambs loud bleat from hilly bourn*, and without sheep *Far From the Madding Crowd* could not exist. If we separate Holman Hunt's sheep from his goats a very different picture emerges. Hunt's *The Hireling Shepherd* and *Our English Coasts* both feature sheep and lambs, strikingly outlined and highlighted in vivid blues and golds without losing any of their innate sheepiness. In the art of Australia and New Zealand, sheep are a regular presence in the landscape – echoing their national mythic significance in both countries no doubt – but goats do not seem to have fired the aesthetic imagination in either country.

Virginia Woolf was known as Goat in her youth (her sister Vanessa was Dolphin). In letters and exchanges with her siblings the family nickname was used humorously and affectionately, but the most poignant recorded instance of *Goat* was Woolf's memory of visiting her mother on her deathbed (Julia Stephen died when Woolf was 14). *This is my last sight of her,* Woolf wrote, *I came to kiss her and as I crept out of the room she said: 'Hold yourself straight, my little Goat.'* Julia Stephen understood the dignity of a goat.

13.

Riroriro,
ruru,
kererū

Those who have studied birds will not find in it anything that they do not already know; those who do not care for birds will not be interested in the subject. So begins Edward Grey's book *The Charm of Birds*, published in 1927. A statement that may say more about the confidence of aristocratic amateurism (the author was, after all, Viscount Grey of Fallodon) than disarming modesty, it still makes me smile, especially as Grey continues in this vein at some length. *Personal observation,* he writes, *will always make a book valuable,* but his observations are *slight and not thorough* and his *opportunities for watching birds have been intermittent.* You have to love a book that works so hard to discourage a reader as Grey's does. Anyway, this chapter comes with a similar disclaimer: if you don't like birds, you should probably skip ahead.

I have been watching the birds around our house on the ridge. From the time I wake in the morning to the last light fading over the paddocks, the birds are a constant presence. I could watch them all day. Some days I do.

When I can't write, or think, or be, when I can't find any reason sufficient to get out of bed – when I *pine for what is not*, as Shelley says in 'To a Skylark' – the birds divert me, take me out of myself. Time slows down and fills up the more the birds absorb my attention. I have no desire to possess them or even touch them (unlike our two Orpington hens, who submit to a gentle stroking of their dense snowy white feathers). Observing the wild birds is enough, following their movement across the sky or their stillness as they perch, watchful, on fence or wire. At night, the morepork hoots constantly from a nearby tree – *MORE-pork*, pause, *MORE-pork* – in a low, falling cadence, so that I wonder when it has time to hunt. During my nights of insomnia, the ruru comforts me; another creature is awake, watching the night too.

But birds are not like me; they don't feel my feelings or share my thoughts. They offer so much more than that. They are utterly other. Even as there are so many clichés about birds, they elude human understanding. Ethereal and ephemeral, they are creatures of contradiction at home in a domain that is barred to humans without the aid of complex modern machinery.

The smallest here, the riroriro, has charmed me since I first heard it over a decade ago in the South Island. Our house then was surrounded by large European trees – oak, chestnut, copper beech – fringing Dunedin's green belt, which is a blend of native bush and introduced species and teeming with bird life. The riroriro weighs almost nothing, only a third the weight of a mouse. An olive-grey bird – with a rounded body above slender black legs, finely pointed black bill and red eyes – it is more often heard than seen, although its habit of hovering makes it identifiable from a distance. I see it now, flying in a fast burst of energy from the safety of one low canopy to another to hop exuberantly among the branches or to flutter above the fern fronds, hunting insects.

The riroriro has a song that carries piercingly through the bush. I had never before heard a bird call like it – a wavering, high-pitched trill, plaintively rising up or falling down the scale. The song of the riroriro transfixes you till it has reached the end of its scale, and keeps you there, waiting, until after a pause it begins over again. Apparently, every riroriro's call is unique, no trill exactly the same – some longer or shorter, some rising, some falling, some varying between the two. As they are found throughout the country, for many people they are the sound of New Zealand. Hearing one on first arriving at our new house in the early summer felt like a benison, but riro means 'gone' in te reo Māori; the bird and its song always suggesting something just lost, just gone, out of sight, like the elusive bird itself. When the poet Ursula Bethell's beloved Effie died, the riroriro featured heavily in Bethell's subsequent commemorative poems mourning Effie's loss.

For the Romantic poets, birds were often not allowed to be birds – they stood in for something else, something the poet considered more important, like art or eternity. Shelley says of his skylark *Bird thou never wert*, while Keats' nightingale is an *immortal Bird*; these poets' birds transcend their bird-ness until they are barely material entities at all. They are capital-B birds. Above all, it was the song, more than the feathered creature, that the poets praised; the birds didn't even need to be visible to the human eye. For me, though, the sight of the bird is as important as its song. The silence with which the black falcon, almost motionless, skims low and slow across the paddock, head down to scan for prey, is an arresting sight, part menace, part beauty – *the achieve of, the mastery of the thing!* as Gerard Manley Hopkins wrote. My body involuntarily mimics the hunting bird's illusion of stillness as, holding my breath, I am unable to avert my gaze even though I know the bird may at any moment plummet to the ground and grasp at something hidden and vulnerable whose death I do not want to witness.

The harrier hawks, too, usually in a pair, glide and circle silently above the open paddocks twice a day, mid-morning and just before dusk, benefiting from the clearing of the land, *the admittance of light to the earth's surface*, and *the increase of creatures which live their lives in the open*, as the nature writer Herbert Guthrie-Smith observed in the late nineteenth century. Some days much closer encounters are possible: roadkill – usually of introduced species like Australian possums or European hedgehogs – provides an easy meal for birds of prey and I have often driven around a curve to surprise a hawk, feasting on a recent traffic victim in the middle of the road, turning its head to regard me with its piercing eye before reluctantly lifting its wings to flap to a roadside tree and wait for the disturbing human presence to drive on. At ground level, the size of the hawk always surprises; it seems to fill the road, more than a match for me. One day, as I was driving along the winding hilltop road to our house, a hawk flew alongside me at eye level, keeping pace with my car along the ridge as I slowed to observe it, human and bird regarding each other for what felt like an age but was only a matter of seconds before it wheeled off to bank down low into the valley.

Not all of the birds here are so portentous, though. The tūī, the R2D2 of honeyeaters with its unique repertoire of sounds – clicks, coughs, grunts, wheezes, whistles and melodic runs of bellbird-like notes – wheels raucously through the branches, staging dogfights with rivals that miraculously avoid collision with other birds or the trees by the smallest of margins, while its wings beat a speedy staccato that sounds like a small engine stuttering. It is also known as the parson-bird because a cluster of white throat feathers contrasts sharply with its black body feathers, resembling the robes of a nineteenth-century minister, but the implication of seriousness could not be more misplaced. With a parrot-like facility for imitation and a lively if not aggressive temperament, tūī are in fact not black but have brown-blue feathers with an iridescent sheen like shot silk when they catch the light, and a dusting of fine white feathers all around their neck in addition to their distinctive throat-frill. One flew into our living room one afternoon – to the amazement of the dog, who was too surprised to do anything other than stare at the flapping, feathered creature. When the tūī was safely returned to the outdoors a few tufts of throat feathers remained behind on the carpet. In the autumn the tūī will retreat to the fruiting rimu trees in the covenanted bush where they can be heard all day but, high in the trees, are rarely seen.

Like the tūī, the kererū combines lustrous feathers with distinctive and entertaining habits of flight. With a small head out of proportion to its large body, the kererū is a bird as drawn by a child but with a stunningly beautiful plumage: snow-white chest, purple iridescence on the wings and a shimmering blue-green on the upper body and tail. During the breeding season the males engage in breathtaking displays of flight: a sharp vertical ascent before suddenly plummeting, wings held out motionless, becoming a mere silhouette of a bird, almost two-dimensional – no mean feat for a bird so portly – seeming to hang in the air but somehow arriving safely at a branch to perch.

Not always though. Kererū can be notoriously clumsy fliers. A kererū once flew at full speed into our picture window in Dunedin with a reverberating thump that made me jump from my armchair next to it. In the time it took me to look up from my book it had managed to fly away, leaving behind a full outline of its collision – wings outstretched, head turned to one side, even the imprint of its beak visible – in the middle of the window pane. Now, the kererū swoop and dive from the tall kahikatea trees in the depths of the bush to a dying kahikatea in the middle of the neighbour's paddock – a daily air-show in the spring and early summer that frequently makes me laugh out loud.

Birds are useful things to think – and to feel – with. Like the bush and the beach, they are part of my recovery just as they are part of my personal history. As Richard Smyth has put it, *We no longer see nature as a child's picture-book; it's more like a challenging Young Adult novel, asking us who we are, what we mean, what we want to be.* Birds pose these questions for me because, in that moment of the encounter – whether the haunting night call of the ruru or the mid-air dancing display of the pīwakawaka – they ground me in a time and place, bring me back to the fullness of the present and banish the distractions of my interior chatter, reducing my thoughts to the elemental. Who am I *here*? What do I want to be *now*?

ᵚ

The days are still as warm as summer, the nights humid and uncomfortable for sleeping, but the first signs of a change of season have begun to appear on the road along our ridge and down the hill to the village. The three poplar trees that stand on a sharp downhill curve, where the full view of the green valley first reveals itself, are just starting to show a burnished tinge to their leaves and this morning, as I drove past, a few fallen leaves swirled golden across the road in my wake.

The kingfishers that have been a daily presence since my arrival at the beginning of summer are no longer in their usual place, sentinels scattered at regular intervals along the power line that hugs the ridge road, on a curve where the bush and tree ferns are at their thickest – Kingfisher Corner, we call it. There are still kingfishers down in the valley, though. I saw one, unusually, in the grass beside the road. Viewed from below, their telltale silhouette – long pointed beak and short body that becomes a darting black arrow in flight – seems in perfect proportion. Seen at ground level, however, their beaks are laughably out of proportion with the rest of their body, like a false beak that you almost expect to see has been cleverly tied on to a much smaller bird, if you weren't distracted by the beauty of the saffron breast feathers against the blue-green brilliance of its wings.

As the autumn progresses, the kingfishers become widespread again and are often seen close to our house, alone or in pairs, sitting on the nearest paddock fence. Although they have not returned to Kingfisher Corner, any drive around the district can now be counted in kingfisher sightings. A trip across the valley towards Kaipara Harbour one Sunday afternoon was a seven-kingfisher drive. On a recent walk the dog discovered a strange sight in the grass by the side of the road: an orange domestic chicken and a kingfisher, both dead, laid out side by side. The two birds were entirely intact, their feathers undisturbed, like a macabre taxidermy display. The dog and I regarded this odd conjunction of species for some minutes. How had they come here? What had brought these birds together in death?

The intermingling of species is not uncommon here, in an environment that blends the indigenous with the introduced and the displaced. Just as I daily hear and see Australian magpies, European pheasants and smaller birds like chaffinches, yellowhammers, goldfinches, blackbirds and the ubiquitous sparrows, so my walks take me past stone pines and eucalyptus trees, the roadside verge blooming with daisies, purple clover and celandines, even wild strawberries. This hybrid environment complicates the question of where I belong. What is this place that feels like home? What is it about this altered landscape, shaped by history as much as nature, that exerts such an emotional pull on me?

✸

In Janet Frame's autobiographical novel *Towards Another Summer*, the protagonist Grace Cleave negotiates her out-of-placeness living in England and her ambivalent feelings about New Zealand by envisioning herself transformed into a bird:

In a way, it was a relief to discover her true identity. For so long she had felt not-human, yet had been unable to move towards an alternative species; now the solution had been found for her; she was a migratory bird ... Why a migratory bird? No doubt because I've journeyed from the other side of the world. Perhaps I'm homesick for my own country and have not realized it. Am I homesick? I haven't thought of my land for so long; my land and my people, that's how it is spoken, like a prayer, the kind that murmurs I possess rather than I want, an arrangement of congratulation between myself and God; I've tried to forget my land and my people ... at least *I'm* not going to write poems and stories which begin *In My Country*, and are filled with nostalgia for 'branches stirring' 'across the moon' – where? At Oamaru, Timaru, Waianakarua? No, that way of thinking and dreaming is not for me.

Frame's clear-eyed interrogation of what it means to belong serves as a kind of mirror image of my own ambivalence about place and home, self and health. Her protagonist experiences England as profoundly alien – its people, its weather, its landscape – but also resists any easy identification with where she came from: constantly asked if she wants to go back home, Grace replies *I was a certified lunatic in New Zealand*, while conceding her attachment *to the rivers and the mountain chains*. The emotional pull of New Zealand's natural environment remains, as well as the literature that frames her response to it: despite Grace's insistence that *that way of thinking and dreaming is not for me*, Frame's novel continues a long association in New Zealand literature with the godwit as a symbol of migratory displacement, from Robin Hyde to Charles Brasch.

England had made me sick, although not certifiably so, and I still thought New Zealand could heal me, make me feel alive again, and provide me with a home where there would be no more sickness – or at least no more homesickness. Nature – bush, birds, beach – seemed the key to this process, if I could just pay attention and read it carefully enough. Could it be unravelled? Or was that a wrong impulse, springing from a desire for a definitive answer or a final destination? Was it the interweaving, the entanglement of time and place, history and self, that I needed to accept? Was that, after all, what home was?

14.

Fitter, happier, more productive

Then the rash returned. So did the insomnia. And the chardonnay.

As the summer had worn on, my runs became shorter, less frequent, my energy sapped by the almost tropical humidity in the north. Easier to lie in bed and read.

I bailed on social invitations. Lunch in the city with two of my favourite former students? Couldn't. Meeting up with one of my oldest university friends who was in New Zealand for a short holiday? Not possible. Barbecue with the new neighbours? Made an excuse.

For several weeks I distracted myself by repainting much of our timber furniture. Obsessively. Bed frames, drawers, dresser, tables large and small. Furniture that had seemed appropriate in the oak-beamed rooms of our thatched house looked heavy and anachronistic in simpler, light-flooded rooms. We couldn't afford to replace it all so I decided to paint it white. Or Paris Grey. Or Aubusson Blue. My husband had already repainted many of the rooms white before I arrived so we were on a joint mission to blot out the past. I wanted to put the darkness behind me.

I failed.

I ran out of things to paint. Dark thoughts began to return, my days became aimless and desultory. After an early swim, I would lose momentum as the day wore on. By the afternoon I would be drowsy, drifting from one half-hearted activity to another, napping too long, trying to avoid thinking and too lazy to do anything useful. I was supposed to be writing a scholarly monograph during my research leave but I was frittering away my time ineffectually.

Imagining life in Matakana while still in England, I had visualised various tableaux: tending my then-hypothetical goats, picking salad greens in the garden, running with the dog on the beach. Maybe I would take up botanical drawing. Or cheese-making. Learn te reo. Join in community tree-planting. I had hoped that this new place would heal me but of course the contents of my head came with me. Now I looked out every day on green bush and field, blue ocean and sky, just as I had imagined. A waxeye hops up the now-wilting flax flower stalk outside my window before darting away.

Now what? I think.

Adam Phillips has described what he calls *our unlived lives – the lives we live in fantasy, the wished-for lives* – and how important they can be for our sense of self. Many of us, Phillips writes, live *a double life, the one that never happens and the one that keeps happening.* For what felt like a long time I had been longing to live elsewhere, live otherwise, but meanwhile the life I was living kept happening. I went to England to live otherwise, only to find that wasn't what I wanted at all. That wasn't home. It didn't feel like my life. My life was elsewhere. Now, back in New Zealand, albeit temporarily, I was still torn between the fantasy of a life and what kept happening. Mine was hardly a unique situation, I knew; ongoing dissatisfaction with daily life is a default position for many with the privilege of choice. As painful and difficult as it might be to make changes, I was lucky that I had the possibility to uproot, to escape, to go home.

This double focus – where I was, where I wanted to be – seemed hard to reconcile because I couldn't resolve the part about what I should be doing. Being at home was a chance to become, and remain, healthy, but life was more than the absence of illness, wasn't it? I needed an occupation beyond feeding goats and walking along the beach.

I had a kind of presentiment that my professional life as I knew it was over. I couldn't see a way back to the research career that used to be my *raison d'être* as an academic – visiting archives and libraries, writing books and articles, speaking at conferences. I had always found ways to snatch hours intended for the more prosaic parts of the job – paperwork, marking – to spend on research and writing. The teaching part of my job had been the price I was willing to pay to do my real work: the research. I would have several projects on the go at once and would still be scanning the internet for the next big conference, the next big idea, the next must-read book in my field. I thrived on the feeling of being slightly overloaded, juggling just a bit more than I could easily handle. It was satisfying and stimulating and reassuring. I could look ahead to a string of upcoming projects and deadlines with keen anticipation. I had a purpose, I had a contribution to make.

Now, none of that seemed important. If I tried to talk about my growing sense of intellectual disengagement to academic friends and colleagues they all assumed that it was the kind of writer's block they knew from their own experience. *Everyone feels that way*, they said, *everyone thinks this is it, this time they won't ever get over it.* If I was honest, though, my writer's block had lasted for a few years. In that time, I had produced some 'outputs', as current university management-speak puts it: chapters, articles, presentations. But I felt they had no spark or freshness and only the most procedural of thinking shoehorned into an argument with some supporting research.

What I couldn't yet determine was whether this was just a lingering symptom of depression. After a year on medication I no longer felt weighed down by a depressive's sense of meaninglessness, but how much could I rely on my feeling that my career was sterile and pointless? Should I trust that niggling sense that I wouldn't truly recover until I acknowledged a fundamental change in myself and entertained other possibilities for my future? What would give my life purpose and how would I even recognise it now that the driving motivation of my adult life – to be a scholar – had seemingly evaporated?

Few other professions, writes Miya Tokumitsu, *fuse the personal identity of their workers so intimately with their work output* as academia. The nebulous boundary between work and not-work is one of the reasons that some of us are so attracted to academia in the first place, but it also makes it harder for us to know when to stop. Of course many other professions face ever-increasing workloads as well, but it is the close identification of the self with the scholar that makes so many academics overwork in a way that does us harm. As the Australian academic Kate Bowles sums up the problem:

> This is the story academics tell ourselves as we flip open the laptop on Sunday mornings: we tell ourselves that the boundarylessness of our time and service is a privilege and even a practice of freedom. Over and over I have heard academics say that they couldn't bear to punch the electronic time clock as our professional colleagues do ... We overwork like cyclists dope: because everyone does it, because it's what you do to get by.

It was no accident, I believe, that my depression first entered its worst phase during my second year in England, after a university term when I had worked seven days a week just to get by, and had not been able to spend a day on research in that time. I don't blame the university for my depression – my past experience, current unhappiness and genetic predisposition tipped me well over that line without any outside assistance.

At the same time, though, all the memoirs of depression I have read talk about how deceitful the illness is. The guilt associated with depression taints every negative feeling. One is never simply sad or disappointed or hurt or angry; negative feelings amplify in the echo chamber of depression. For the first time in my adult life, once I moved to England I started to think about leaving academia, but I worried that I was self-sabotaging from the outset. How could I expect to adapt to migration and all the change it brought if I was feeling so conflicted about my career? I shouldn't feel sad, wasn't this job what I had always wanted? I shouldn't feel disappointed, people would kill for this position. I shouldn't feel hurt or angry about professional setbacks, I just had to face the fact that I wasn't as clever as I should be and I was lucky to have made it this far in my career with such mediocre abilities. I just had to work harder.

ᴡ

Driving to Ōmaha beach on a morning still warm enough for swimming, I suddenly tuned in to one of those multiple tracks constantly playing in my mind. *Hurry up or you'll miss out.* On what, exactly? Did I think the beach was going to be used up before I got there? But this track was always playing, whatever I was doing or thinking, however insignificant.

Hurry up or someone else will finish first and earn the teacher's praise.

Hurry up or someone else will buy the house you've set your heart on. Make an offer today.

Hurry up and get promoted before somebody else does.

Hurry up or someone else will be better than you, take what you want, achieve more.

It was odd, though, to hear it now, so distinctly, on my way to the beach for a swim. Where had I picked up that message? How had it embedded so deep? What would be so bad about not hurrying all of those things? What would missing out mean?

FOMO – fear of missing out – is a cultural meme that has already become passé, such is the accelerated pace of social media, but that has not stopped the phenomenon becoming the subject of academic study, where it is defined as *a pervasive apprehension that others might be having rewarding experiences from which one is absent.* Long before Instagram, however, I was cultivating FOMO from a young age. I did my best to rein in my habitual tendency towards impatience and ambition with the self-denial encouraged by my evangelical upbringing. By my early 30s, however, as the mother of a small child and in precarious academic employment, I felt that I had already missed out, that I would never catch up. Overachievement was the only achievement that counted, and when I couldn't succeed on those terms anything else felt like failure. I had made up some ground during my years in Dunedin, which had led to my job in England, but once there I faltered, unable to sustain the pace and intensity of work that I felt was required. The reality was that my career no longer gave me satisfaction; if I stopped identifying so closely with my job, who would I be?

15.

Still ill

I wake early in my uncurtained bedroom each day. From the first blush of dawn, the day presents a spectacular display: golden shafts of light suffusing dove-grey cloudheads, or the shocking pinks and oranges of the sun breaking the blue horizon with dazzling force. Some days the distant islands in the gulf are sharply distinct, their contours clearly traceable; sometimes they are just an indigo mass, partially obscured by low cloud; other days they are hidden from sight completely, merged with the hazy shades of blue that blend sky, sea and land into a single entity beyond the green rolling hills in the foreground.

Dawn brings out the birds – tūī in the flax, swallows swooping under the eaves in pursuit of moths, or waxeyes who land on the verandah railing and regard me warily before darting off again. The harrier hawk makes her low, slow circuits of the paddocks, head down and eye fixed for any movement or shadow in the long grass, while the small birds in the undergrowth twitter in agitation as they detect her unwanted proximity.

Then perhaps an early drive to the beach, just for a run or a walk if the morning is too cool to swim. One morning I had to stop the car for a pheasant hen and her three chicks to cross the road. Another day two Californian quails pecked in the shade by the side of the road. As I descend from the ridge into the fertile valley below, the sight of the green pastured hillocks, the stand of oaks lining the road, the scattered fruit trees dotted with lemons or apples, the rusty barns and faded red milking sheds, is like a template for the antipodean picturesque. The temperature rises in the sheltered valley, full of the promise of another warm day, although the air on our hilltop is still fresh and cool with the heavy dew.

And then what?

I cook. I knit. I read read read. *I read the way a person might swim, to save her or his life*, as Mary Oliver wrote. But I don't sleep. I don't write. I drink too much. I gain weight. I brood. The thoughts circle circle circle.

Because after the present comes the future.

To think about death at a time like this shows a distinct lack of imagination. Nonetheless, that is what I do.

Even though I now experience moments of searing happiness, almost overcome by the beauty of this new place, I can't entirely shake myself free of suicidal thoughts. The delusion of depression whispered, *wouldn't it be wonderful to die now and never have to experience the depths again?* I did not hear nightingales in the bush but *easeful Death* had an appeal I could not explain and would never dare to disclose.

It's to die for. A cringeworthy cliché used by advertisers and real estate agents. It could be a sea view or a new kitchen but it is something so wonderful, so satisfying that there is nothing left to experience. Having attained it, consumed it, one is replete and would happily die. I can't speak for other depressives, but the phrase always chills me and I have never uttered it myself. It's too close to the bone. Now I was surrounded by the kind of beauty and comfort and tranquillity that I used to crave. So was it all to die for? Or could I find a way to live in it, for it?

During my binge reading of depression memoirs, I was constantly puzzled by the gap, the missing link, between the first part of the book – the compelling gothic details of the descent into depression, illness, madness, call it what you will – and the usually much shorter as well as less interesting section on recovery. As the depressed author began to improve, there was often a switch to a responsible, community-service-type voice (*statistics show that depression rates are rising exponentially …* *if you or someone you know suffers from depression …*) and the palpable immediacy of their stories started to recede. The authors expressed gratitude to understanding spouses or supportive therapists, mentioned helpful practices like swimming or meditation. But I always finished their books feeling I never quite understood how the author had made it to recovery from the depths of despair so colourfully depicted.

So for all my reading, as well as my previous experience, it was only after I had been back in New Zealand for a few months that I began to realise that I was not yet well. While my OCD had improved, obsessive thoughts about contamination were still a daily presence. I was realistic and had not expected a full recovery; I just wanted the OCD to be more manageable and not inhibit so much of normal life. But I had genuinely thought I was over my depression. I didn't feel sad; I had lots of good days.

I wanted to believe I was better because – from a distance – I looked like a functioning adult. I was easier to live with. I was less withdrawn from domestic routines than I had been for a long time; my husband was no longer having to complete all the household cleaning and shopping, which had fallen entirely to him in England when my OCD was at its most incapacitating. And I'm sure he wanted to believe I was better, too; he had never complained but I know I had been a killjoy to live with.

So, when I had first arrived back in New Zealand, we both subscribed to the *Wendy has recovered* fiction. We didn't talk about my illness. He had been through all this with me once before – the breakdown and recovery in my thirties – and this plot was becoming repetitive. With our shared love of narratives, we were both ready to move on to the next part of the story: *and then we returned to New Zealand and everything was fine again, as if the last three years had never happened. Look, here we are lying on the beach after a swim on a Saturday morning instead of battling ring-road traffic to Waitrose, how lucky are we? Look, here we are lunching at a local winery instead of a drab English café. Can't you breathe the serenity? Isn't life good?*

And it was. But I was still a depressive with OCD.

ϒ

Today started out well enough. I had enough time to read in bed with my toast and coffee before driving my son to meet his school bus down in the village. From there I drive to the beach to run along the track through the dunes because the tide is too high to run on the sand. I stop for a few minutes at the end of the track, at a wooden bench beneath the headland, where the full sweep of the beach unfolds before you. The high tide completely covers the rock platform that I had walked on two days earlier at the same time of day. This morning there is only water, sky and sand as I look north, with my back to the green headland. None of the dog walkers have ventured this far along the beach so I have the point to myself, and an oystercatcher or two.

After my run I stop in the village on the way home for another coffee, watching the first signs of life on a quiet weekday. Parents walking their kids to school. Tradies and shop workers picking up a takeaway latte to get them through to their first break of the morning.

Once home, I scoop fermented barley – reeking, as usual – into three buckets for the goats and walk down to their paddock, where I do my best to ensure each has roughly the equivalent amount. Pansy butts the smaller two out of the way from time to time, but so intent is she on checking she is not missing out on anything that the others – Myrtle in particular – always manage to get their fair share by quiet persistence and a watchful eye on any sudden movement from Pansy's horns. Myrtle likes to kneel at her barley bucket, while Marjoram is still a little skittish, always the first to shy away in alarm and the least likely to consent to a few pats when the barley is all gone.

Checking the chicken coop for eggs (none today), I return to the house for a shower and then complete two loads of laundry, hanging sheets, towels and tablecloths in the morning sun to dry.

From there, the day unravels. I can't settle to any reading. Despite my caffeine intake and a reasonable sleep the night before, I am drowsy and lethargic. I potter at a few inconsequential domestic tasks, wander out to the verandah to look at the view. I come back inside and try a different book. I doze briefly. It's 11am. I think about the writing commitments and administrative duties that still hang over me, having followed me from England, but feel powerless and inept as if I have been asked to complete a report in a language I have never heard spoken. *And if I can't complete such relatively simple tasks,* my mind continues, *how can I do anything productive with my life?* How long can I keep procrastinating, agonising, before conceding defeat?

By 11.30 I am thinking about death again. I have a car and an empty house until the end of the day. I have bush beyond my boundary fence where no one would see me or know where I had gone.

Despair makes me hungry so I eat an early lunch then go back to lying on my bed with the sleeping dog. Hours pass as I look at every side of thoughts that crystallise as

> *worthless*
> *pointless*
> *wasted*
> *failure.*

By 2.30 I am wondering if I should call my husband (*can you come home? I don't think I should be by myself*) but imagine him feeling mystified (*she seemed fine this morning*), hearing my plaintive voice on the phone while he scans his desk seeing an afternoon's work that can't easily be cast aside.

I don't call.

Instead I search the internet for a local psychotherapist and make an appointment for a week's time. *Is that OK?* she asks on the phone. *Yes,* I say casually, *no problem,* as if I have no pressing need for help but just want a bit of a chat about the meaning of life. *I can wait a week,* I say.

I eat some ice-cream. I don't even really *like* ice-cream but I have been eating a lot of it this summer.

I walk back down to the goat paddock. From the house they are out of sight, but I hear their bells coming from the small grove of mānuka trees in the bottom corner of the paddock. They look surprised to see me but after sniffing my hands they return to grazing or scratching their horns against the low branches. Myrtle sits down between two small trees. Marjoram joins her. I would like to settle down with them there too; instead I leave them to their goaty business and go back to the house to wait out the afternoon till the family arrives home.

It's a hot afternoon. Maybe I'll have a cold beer. And some crackers.

That's another day gone.

16.

I said
no,
no,
no

I flunked out of rehab after 24 hours.

I had visited the Retreat two weeks earlier for a tour and an interview with the director, Agnes. She was warm and welcoming, the Retreat tastefully decorated, more like a luxury B&B than a residential facility, overlooking a beautiful valley dotted with sheep and alive with birdsong.

My relapse had been swift and scary. The bad days had started to outnumber the good until it seemed like one day I was doing the usual things – swimming, reading, cooking, walking the dog, talking to the goats – and the next I had retreated to bed, feeling the abyss opening beneath me again. No matter how long I gazed at the ocean, I couldn't shake the suffocating sense of hopelessness closing in on me. I needed to do something, take some urgent and radical action to stop this decline in its tracks. Enough. No more.

I googled retreats, clinics for treating depression or OCD, wellness centres offering personal transformation through yoga, meditation and cleanses. They were all eye-wateringly expensive but *this was an emergency*. I didn't want to die. I wanted to recover. I wanted this to be over. What I was currently doing, what I had hoped would be sufficient to cure me, had failed. I couldn't see a future like this. So I emailed Agnes and, after a pleasant phone chat, I drove to a rural valley west of Auckland to visit the women-only Retreat and see if it felt like the right place.

Following her directions, I turned off the main road and found myself on a long driveway winding through the cool stillness of a stand of majestic tōtara trees. Their dappled shade and thick foliage cut off any sense of the other houses and the village school that I had just passed on the road, so when the Retreat residence appeared at the end of the driveway it was as if one had literally retreated from the world. Agnes came out to meet me with a motherly hug. I took a deep breath and felt the first prickling of hope.

In a way, I didn't know why I had come here; we could not possibly afford the three-week stay for the treatment programme at the Retreat but my husband had said, *We will find the money somehow, if you feel it is what you need to do.* The private hospital programmes I had investigated were almost twice the cost of the Retreat so here I was, feeling guilty at the prospect of totally depleting our finances but, at the same time, thinking that keeping alive was worth whatever it cost, surely?

Agnes showed me the house (*This would be your room*, she said, taking me into a large, light bedroom, decorated in neutral tones, with sweeping valley views) and the garden. We then returned to the living room and, after a long talk over excellent coffee, Agnes walked with me to my car and said, *Give it some thought and let me know your decision.* I drove home having already decided to proceed. The extremity of the step – committing to residential treatment – felt like an acknowledgement of how bad a state I was in. *If I do this*, I thought, *it shows how committed I am to recovery.* Wouldn't such a leap of faith be rewarded? I informed family, friends, and colleagues of what I was about to do – I wanted to be completely open about my condition, no looking back, no half-measures any more. I came out loud and proud as a phobic depressive with OCD who was going to do something about it, finally, definitively.

Having made this decision, I was keen to check in immediately but I needed to wait a week before the Retreat could admit me. I also had to have a pre-admission assessment by another consultant psychologist, Agnes had said, *so that we can tailor a programme specific to your needs.*

The consultant psychologist's office was above a large furniture store in inner-city Auckland. Following a wide corridor past offices occupied by law firms and the kind of IT companies that feature the word 'Solutions' in their name, I arrived at the locked door of a darkened office. The psychologist was late and it was clearly a one-man operation; no receptionist on hand to greet nervous clients, no waiting room. Standing in a corridor, breathing that chemical smell of synthetic carpet and industrial cleaning products, I felt like I was waiting to meet a slightly shady private investigator. I could see into the neighbouring office – occupied by Moonstone Ministries, New Zealand Division – where all seemed calm, no urgent demands to minister to the spiritually ailing today, evidently. On the other side, by contrast, the graphic designers were a hum of nervous activity – *Rhonda, what's the latest you can drop off those designs today?* – suggesting tight margins and demanding clients.

After fifteen minutes, Todd the psychologist breezed in, apologising profusely as he unlocked the office door, turning on the lights and a small pedestal fan – he was sweating from a hot drive across the city – before sitting in an armchair with a folder and pen and gesturing me to another chair opposite him. I could see him visibly gather himself, turn his professional attention to me and attempt to create an air of stillness after his heated rush. I was nervous, as I always am at a first meeting like this – *time to spill your guts, again, but in a concise and ordered way within the time constraints* – but I also wondered about his day. How many demands on his sympathy had already been made by one o'clock in the afternoon? I tried to suppress my sartorial judgement about the kind of Velcro-ed sandals he was wearing. *Don't be so shallow. Dress sense is no reliable indicator of a person's wisdom about the human condition.*

He smiled, with what felt like genuine warmth, and began by congratulating me on *taking this first step towards recovery.* I must have looked confused because he frowned then looked down at his notes before asking, *You are entering addiction recovery, aren't you?*

No. I have depression, contamination phobia and OCD, I said.

Just garden-variety disorders, not the hint of tawdry celebrity glamour attached to substance addiction, I thought but did not say. I knew that the Retreat was most commonly a haven for recovering alcoholics but it also advertised its services for the treatment of depression and anxiety, which was why it had caught my eye in the first place. And it wouldn't hurt to knock my penchant for chardonnay on the head while I was at it, I had thought. Three weeks without alcohol would be useful to clarify the mind.

Todd apologised again. *Well,* he said, *well done, anyway, for seeking treatment.*

My heart sank.

As the session continued, though, Todd was thoughtful, listening carefully, taking his time to find the right word or image to capture an idea or convey an insight to me. He heard the grief in my voice when I spoke about losing my ambition and my love for my job. He expressed concern about my isolation, lacking a wider network of support or friendship beyond my immediate family. I left feeling reassured that his report to Agnes would provide an accurate sense of my current state and that, as a result, I would be in good hands.

The following Monday my husband drove me to the Retreat (there was a rule that clients could not leave their own cars on site so I had to be dropped off). Agnes showed me to my room and asked me to join her for lunch on the deck when I was ready. Firstly, though, she needed to confiscate both my phone and my laptop as internet access or outside communication were against the rules. I had been under the impression that I could keep my laptop with me, provided I agreed not to connect to wi-fi, so that I could continue with my writing – but apparently the only writing I would be doing for the next three weeks was in my Retreat Workbook.

That was the first warning sign.

The second was at lunch when it became clear that I was the only *guest* currently in residence at the Retreat and that this would continue for the duration of my stay. Once a three-week programme was under way, no-one else could be admitted part way through.

All of my meals would therefore be *à deux* with Agnes and all of my sessions would be one-on-one, either with Agnes or a second on-site psychologist, Brenda.

After a lunch of small talk in the sunshine, I became aware that I was feeling utterly exhausted, as if I had arrived at the Retreat after a 30-hour flight, reeling from jet lag. I was numb and disoriented. I found it difficult to concentrate when we adjourned to the lounge to go through some preliminaries concerning the schedule and the workbook. No doubt seeing my glazed expression, Agnes suggested I go for a nap and we could pick up again later in the afternoon. I agreed and she said she would come to my room to wake me at four. (*Bedroom doors to remain open, please.*)

At four, feeling unrefreshed but no longer quite so sedated, I rejoined Agnes and we recommenced where we had left off. My pre-admission visit had not given me an accurate sense of what the schedule would be and it appeared that the day would be full, from 7am onwards, with only an hour's free time between 4 and 5pm, but as there seemed to be a lot of expectation regarding homework in the workbook it was hard to see how I would find any breathing space. Or reading space. I had brought a carry-on bag full of books, in addition to my suitcase of clothes, in the hope that I would have time for a range of reading. Warning sign no. 3.

Dinner was served early at the Retreat because, according to the schedule, *every evening Agnes and I would attend an AA meeting* somewhere in the district. I knew that many women who came to the Retreat had alcohol issues but I had seriously underestimated the extent to which the entire programme was based on a 12-step addiction treatment model that included compulsory AA meetings. I had assumed that the *individually tailored programme* I had been promised would focus on depression, anxiety and OCD, rather than alcohol, which I thought was a side issue rather than the main problem. *No*, said Agnes, *all of our ladies benefit from AA meetings. And you should really surrender your hand sanitiser to me as we do not allow any alcohol at all on the premises.* There was no way I was handing that over. We agreed to come back to that issue later.

By this point (warning sign no. 4), the walls had definitely started to close in on me. I was keeping up a cheerful front, I hoped, behaving more like an obliging house guest than an inpatient suffering from depression, but the fact that we had not yet commenced *any real work*, as Agnes put it, was a cause for concern to us both. I wanted – I thought – to get stuck into the programme straight away, but I could not shake this feeling of detachment and the surreal air of a Retreat solely devoted to me. Agnes said that it was understandable I was feeling a bit overwhelmed and I would no doubt feel better tomorrow. I hoped she was right.

That first evening, Klaus the chef served a delicious meal of lamb with spiced aubergine and wilted spinach. I was famished and savoured every mouthful, feeling restored and comforted by the hot meal after the strange disquiet I had been unable to dispel since arriving. I think if I had been able to spend a quiet evening alone then things might have turned out differently, but immediately after our early dinner Agnes drove me to my first AA meeting, back in the centre of the city.

She chatted animatedly through the 40-minute drive but I was so far out of my depth at this point that it was as if I was looking down at myself in her car from a great height. *Who was this person wearing my clothes on her way to an AA meeting as if it was no big deal? How did I get here? How could I get out of here?*

I had watched enough films and TV programmes to know what to expect at the meeting. Truth be told, I have rather an obsession with rehab movies and books, however cheesy. I love the salvation stories they offer; the camaraderie that inevitably develops among the ill-suited mix of patients; the group therapy sessions sitting in a circle – at first humorous and played for laughs and then suddenly profound as the silent member finally speaks; the tragedy of someone's relapse and death (someone always dies) before our heroine sees the light and finds her way.

The shabby church hall with strip lighting and plastic chairs to which Agnes brought me was straight out of *Breaking Bad*. There was instant coffee in plastic cups, into which several young men were stirring multiple spoonfuls of sugar. There were AA banners, displaying the 12 Steps and the Serenity Prayer, in an archaic font similar to that I remembered from childhood when my family had attended Christian Mission tent meetings. Suited professionals, elderly people who would look at home in any Sunday congregation and street dwellers all greeted each other warmly over a smoke outside the hall, or milling about in the rows of seats before the meeting formally commenced. Over the hubbub, Agnes said to me, *You won't have to say anything, you can just observe.* She meant to reassure me but I only felt more out of place as the meeting got under way and the chairwoman asked if there was *anyone here for the first time tonight?* Agnes caught my eye and subtly shook her head. A couple of people put up their hands and were clapped and welcomed by the regulars. I sat in silence, eyes down, feeling like an imposter, an interloper.

Mostly, though, I was still trembling after the unexpected greeting from one of the less well-groomed members, who had taken me unawares and shaken my hand heartily when I arrived. All through the meeting, I was aware of my right hand, not yet sufficiently decontaminated, as I had only had time for a surreptitious dab of hand sanitiser before the meeting began. I would need to wash and sanitise my hand several times more when I returned to the Retreat before I could calm down properly. And I needed to be aware of everything I touched until then as they, too, would need a clean up (my handbag, my glasses, my cardigan).

Proceedings commenced. After preliminaries, the chairwoman announced that tonight's meeting would focus on Step Two, that *only a Power greater than ourselves could restore us to sanity.* Well-thumbed copies of the AA Big Book had been placed on every seat and she suggested we go around the room, each person reading aloud a paragraph from the chapter devoted to Step Two. Agnes frowned. Apparently this was not a typical meeting format and she seemed concerned that it was not providing a good introduction for me. By this point I could not have felt any more uncomfortable if they had started passing around pieces of raw chicken for us to lick, but I tried to look calm and willed the meeting to be over.

The reading was excruciating as readers stumbled over the dated style and proselytising message of the Big Book. (*We have found much of heaven and we have been rocketed into a fourth dimension of existence of which we had not even dreamed.*) A few, like me, shook their heads, declining to read aloud, and there would be an awkward pause and a momentary confusion as the next reader took up their task before they had been expecting it. It seemed to last forever. It must have taken 20 minutes.

Then the sharing commenced and the whole atmosphere of the room changed, as if a window had been thrown open on a summer's day. One after another, from different points around the room, people spoke with eloquence and humility about their struggles to believe; the desperation with which – as a last resort – they had appealed to a Higher Power, however they conceived it; their continuing battle to stave off despair or relapse, and cling to some kind of hope that change was possible. Few seemed to have had any previous experience or knowledge of religion, some reported that they were hostile or indifferent to it, but all who shared related how, in their extremity, they had tried something entirely unfamiliar, hopelessly old-fashioned, out of step with everything they previously knew.

I was deeply moved by the sharers' willingness to expose themselves in this way, to make themselves vulnerable, as they described their attempts to connect with the ineffable, the beyond-self, however they understood it. Their language broke free of the flowery clichés of the Big Book; they spoke in vivid images and with a refreshing spontaneity. Listening to these people entirely disengaged my default mode of critique concerning religion, resulting from my childhood immersion in fundamentalism. I was captivated and would have willingly listened to such sharing for the rest of the evening, but the meeting ended all too quickly and Agnes and I made a hasty exit. In the car, she was keen to impress upon me that this had been an unusual meeting, that she herself had serious reservations about the Higher Power aspect of AA, and that she was disappointed with the chairwoman for devoting so much time to this one aspect of the 12 Steps.

Once back at the Retreat I had homework to complete in the workbook before I could go to bed. After the day, and especially after the sensory overload of the meeting, I was utterly depleted and reluctantly opened up the folder to the Day One section. Just looking at the columns headed *Benefits of Today* and *Deficits of Today* froze my thought processes and I knew I would not be able to write a word. So I looked ahead to the next module, Day Two, in the hope that would be more encouraging, and saw that I would be called upon to describe

– in a single paragraph – *How my life has become unmanageable* (Step One of the 12-Step Programme) and *Provide an example that illustrates how my life has become unmanageable.* My mental inertia locked solid.

I put the workbook aside and turned out the light. I lay awake most of the night.

17.

Today
I will
do
one
thing

At seven the next morning Agnes appeared in her dressing gown and placed a steaming flat white on my bedside table, before opening the curtains of my room to reveal the morning sun breaking through the towering eucalypts across the valley. I was extremely grateful for the coffee but there was something buzzing at the corner of my mind, something that disturbed and unsettled me. Something to do with Agnes in my room.

Guests (i.e. me) needed to be woken at seven for Reflection, scheduled for 7 to 7.30am each day before breakfast. I had been instructed to read one of the daily meditations from a small book Agnes had provided, reflect on it, and then share my thoughts with her at the beginning of our discussion in the first formal session of the morning. Unfortunately, the small book had all the wisdom and profundity of the average desk calendar, featuring a smorgasbord of inspirational quotations from self-help gurus such as Friedrich Nietzsche.

I had lost count of which number warning sign I was up to at this point.

After skimming through a large number of the page-long entries – all toe-curlingly simplistic and sentimental – I decided that I needed to be honest about my response. If I wanted this treatment programme to work, I would have to overcome my good-girl tendency (which was already deserting me, anyway – when had I ever *not* completed assigned homework?) and speak the truth about my misgivings so far. Surely Agnes would respect my honesty? Surely it was reasonable to expect that the individually tailored programme I had been promised could be adapted in some way?

After breakfast, Agnes and I sat across the table from each other, both with our large workbook folders open in front of us.

Can we start by you reading aloud to me the reflection you looked at this morning? Agnes said.

I paused. I hadn't expected that request. In my room, I had hit upon a page that, if all else failed, I could claim as my morning reflection as it was based on the Serenity Prayer and, after last night's meeting, I had been reconsidering this well-known affirmation in a new light.

But I absolutely couldn't read it aloud.

I have read aloud ever since I learned to read. To myself as a child, if there was no one else around to read to me, or just for the sound of the words on the page. To my children, in that familiar bedtime ritual, everything from *One Fish, Two Fish, Red Fish, Blue Fish* to *The Lion, the Witch and the Wardrobe*. To my students, to draw their attention to a passage in a novel they might have skimmed over too quickly, to remind them that we were studying words and language, not simply stories or themes.

But there was no way I could now find a voice to read that page to Agnes. It felt infantilising, demeaning. It would force me to give voice to statements that I found glibly superficial, that I did not want to claim.

The silence stretched between us. Agnes looked puzzled.

Can you read it for me, Wendy? she repeated.

No. No, I can't do that. I'm sorry. My heart was thumping. Why was I making such a big thing of this? Why couldn't I just go along with it for now and hope that I would start to feel less awkward and out of place here?

But this is how we start the day. If you don't begin this way, then we cannot follow the programme.

I tried, then, to explain how the reflections book alienated me. It wasn't how I think. I was used to reading about ideas, theories of body and mind. I could not relate to affirmations presented so shallowly. Life was complex. Being alive was complex. That complexity needed affirming, not reducing to the lowest common denominator.

Well, Agnes said. *There are plenty of other books down in the library. Let's go and look and see if there is something else that suits you better.*

So we walked downstairs to the library alcove where she showed me a shelf filled with a series of the small books just like the one she had given me already, published by a famous treatment centre, their spines in a variety of pastel colours and with similar titles like *Each Day a New Beginning, The Promise of a New Day, Today I Will Do One Thing.*

The walls closed in some more.

No, I said, *I don't think these would be any different.*

Now I sensed a slight annoyance from Agnes that she was trying to mask. Had no-one else ever challenged her in this way?

We went back to sit at the table again. She took a deep breath and said, *We will not be able to do our work together if you can't accept the programme. This is the way we work here. If you don't do the reading and do your homework, you won't get better. You have made a big investment coming here. Let's take a short break while you think about that.*

Stung, I went outside to breathe in some fresh air. *Bad girl, bad girl, bad girl,* the voice in my head said. What was happening? Was I sabotaging myself again? Was this just resistance, the last attempt by the sick part of my psyche to hold on to the status quo? Was I so scared of recovery, of having to delve deeper into the pain, the darkness, the badness, that my mind was doing whatever it could to avoid it, to keep me safe, in some perverse way? Were my symptoms a weird form of protection that I was utterly afraid of giving up?

Yes.

But.

Was it too much to ask that I could be given some space to acclimatise, that I could be eased in to the programme more, that

I could be treated by someone who valued the way I thought, rather than dismissing it as part of my problem? Yes, I know I *over-intellectualise* but I can't leave my brain at the door when I seek treatment. Some of the greatest writers and thinkers have suffered from depression, anxiety, madness, so there is a vast wealth of resources out there from people who have imaginatively explored their problems and their cures, their relapses and their recoveries. Why did mental health professionals rarely draw on this? If mental illness was complex and multilayered why did treatment always seem to be so facile?

I didn't want to go back into the house. Instead, I wandered up the driveway, in among the trees, where I immediately felt calmer, clearer, refreshed. I wanted to stay there but suddenly Brenda's car appeared ahead of me. I was scheduled to have my first session with her at 10am. She parked her car and went in to see Agnes where, no doubt, she would be informed of my recalcitrance.

Brenda's office was in a small building a short distance away from the main house. She had been with Agnes for 15 minutes so we were late starting my session, but as we slowly walked up the path to the office, Brenda made small talk about the weather and the traffic snarl she had been caught in. She was a woman of my own age with a healthy tan and a stylish pixie cut, immaculately turned out in a burnt orange silk jacket over a tailored linen dress. Her pedicure, peeping through the high-heeled sandals she wore, perfectly matched the colour of her jacket. Brenda's orange toenails took my attention repeatedly through the session that followed.

We began with a questionnaire regarding my alcohol consumption, the third I had taken since arriving the day before. None of the results were ever disclosed to me but I had the impression that they were below what both Agnes and Brenda had expected. I was never tested for depression or anxiety, not that I set much store by such schematic tests, but it struck me as odd that no attention was given to my primary symptoms in this way.

Brenda then embarked on a long introduction about how difficult it can be to start intensive therapy like this, intended to reassure me but in fact having the effect of silencing me. The longer she talked and the more she encouraged me to commit to the programme with anecdotes of successful outcomes with previous residents, the less I felt seen or heard. How was it, I thought, that I was alone at this Retreat but both Brenda and Agnes made me feel like I wasn't there? That unless I behaved like a good Retreater, there was no place for me here at all? And why did they keep banging on about alcohol when my biggest fear at the moment was that I might deliberately drive my car off the top of our ridge one day, stone cold sober?

I wanted to say to Brenda: *I have painted toes. I have jackets and tailored dresses. I'm a professional woman too.*

I didn't say anything. I was embarrassed to realise that, even if I didn't express it, I felt the need to impress Brenda. I was here for recovery. I was off-duty. I was wearing the comfortable clothes I had been told to bring. But I felt inadequate, silently judged, as I always did when in the presence of a stylish woman.

Brenda was not without insight and a couple of things she said struck a chord with me so that I felt I could well up if she pushed on in that direction, but instead she ploughed on to another point, another digression, taking my thoughts down a different path, away from the painful point she had exposed. I struggled a bit to keep up as she continued talking but it didn't seem to matter as she didn't call on me to respond. Afterwards, I thought she and Agnes must have decided I needed a pep talk to get me on board with the programme; it felt more like I had spent an hour with a motivational speaker than an hour in therapy.

Finally, Brenda sent me back to the main house to re-join Agnes. I dawdled, stopping to watch Agnes' chickens as they scoured the chookyard for insects, scratching at the dirt and bending their heads low to closely inspect what they had uncovered beneath their feet.

Agnes was waiting for me on the sunny deck at the back of the house. She made me coffee (again) and we talked in a low-key way, but inside, through the open French doors, I could see the table with our workbooks where we had left them.

It's been a tough morning, she said, *so we'll have an early lunch and then try and make up the ground we lost this morning.*

I don't think I had yet formulated the thought, *I want to go home.*
I felt extremely uncomfortable, not at ease in my skin or in this place
where I was neither really a guest nor a patient. In one sense nothing
much was going on, but at the same time I felt drained, trying not to
think ahead to the next session or the next evening meeting, hoping
that some switch would be turned on so I could engage with the
process and feel I was making some headway.

But something happened on our way in from lunch on the
deck back to the room with the worktable. I must have looked as
uncomfortable and on edge as I felt because Agnes suddenly turned to
me and said, *It's not working, is it?*

I was taken aback. The next thing I recall is that we were sitting
on the sofas by the fireplace, where we had sat for our talk on my
preliminary visit to the Retreat, and Agnes was saying, *If you can't
commit to the process, this won't work. You need to commit to your recovery.
I'm here to help you but you have to want to see it through. I can't do it for
you. You need to do your homework and follow the workbook. That is what
we do here; that's what the programme is. You can't pick and choose the bits
you want to do, you have to sign up for all of it. Your recovery depends on it.
Maybe you're not as ready for recovery as you thought you were?*

I smarted at this judgement. What happened to the *individual
programme tailored to your needs*? Why was I receiving what felt like an
ultimatum after less than a day? And why did I sense that, beneath the
'tough-love' professional exterior that Agnes was projecting, she was
just plain cross with me?

Oh, I get it. I was the naughty child wearing out the patience of
the busy grown-up. The cause of the unease that had niggled at me
this morning when Agnes came into my room was now suddenly
obvious. She was the chatty, full-figured woman who I was alone with
much of the day, organising my time and my meals, deciding when I
went to bed and when I woke up, telling me what to do. And I was
suffocating. I wanted to run as far and as fast as I could so I could
breathe. But in the meantime, I could refuse to cooperate. In fact, I
had no choice because I felt numb. And blank.

18.

A
hole
in the
heart

Whenever therapists have asked me about my relationship with my
mother – which they invariably do – I have always shrugged it off.
We're not close, I say. *No, I don't remember a time when we were close.* There
was just a blankness, nothing there to talk about, nothing to feel.

But one day, while researching an article I was trying to write
about the figure of the vulnerable child in Dickens, I read an essay
about the mother–child relationship by the French psychoanalyst
André Green and something weird happened. I started to tremble,
almost tingle, as Green described not the literal death of the mother
but a sudden loss of the mother's attention and care during early
childhood (typically, due to the mother's own depression or grief).
As Green explains it, the dead mother is *a mother who remains alive but
who is, so to speak, psychically dead in the eyes of the young child in her care.*
On the surface, life may seem to go on as normal between mother
and child but something fundamental has shifted, the mother is simply
going through the motions; *her heart is not in it*, as the cliché goes.

Green hypothesised that this experience in early childhood may be the underlying cause of a distinct form of depression in adult life, not just the usual *sinister black of depression* but *a blank mourning, a blank anxiety* (playing on the meaning of *blanc* in French as a contrast to the darkness of the depressed state) that manifests as a feeling of emptiness and emotional detachment. The child of *the dead mother*, Green suggests, has no way to account for what has happened. To compensate for the perceived loss of the mother's love, the child develops various survival techniques and these inadequate (because childish) techniques can linger into adulthood and impact negatively on the adult's capacity to feel and connect positively with others. Firstly, the child withdraws her feelings of attachment, resulting in what Green evocatively calls *a hole in the texture* of the relationship with the mother, as if the fabric is rent, leaving deep but hidden frayed edges around a hole where love should be.

❦

Up until the age of 15, I was told by successive doctors that I had a hole in the heart resulting from undetected rheumatic fever as a small child. I was a sickly child prone to secondary infections and I spent far too much time bedridden with bronchitis, ear infections, tonsillitis, pneumonia, pleurisy. So it was plausible that I could have suffered a bout of rheumatic fever that was misdiagnosed at the time, resulting in heart damage (as in fact had happened to a cousin of mine).

Wendy has a hole in the heart had been the explanatory myth of my childhood, accounting for my frequent illnesses, lack of stamina, propensity to feel the cold. I never really understood what it meant, in physiological terms; I don't recall it ever being explained to me, or maybe it was and I just didn't understand so it didn't stick in my mind. To a child so steeped in stories, I probably made sense of it in my own way, akin to the fairy tale about the boy with the shard of ice in his heart.

It was only at 15, when the heart is assumed to be fully grown, that it was possible to see a heart specialist and be tested definitively. I *did not have a hole in the heart*, the cardiologist pronounced; I merely had heart valves that did not close efficiently, creating a slight 'whooshing' sound that could be heard via stethoscope (likely to be more pronounced if I was nervous, as I usually was in a doctor's surgery); this minor issue was not uncommonly mistaken for the far more serious condition.

But by 15 the idea of a hole in the heart had taken root, it was part of my identity. It made me special, if vulnerable. Now, apparently, I had been whole all along. No hole, just lazy valves. That wasn't special. The family anecdote would now become *We used to think Wendy had a hole in the heart and then we found out she didn't.*

The second way that the child tries to cope with the perceived loss of the dead mother's love, André Green proposed, is that the child will instead try to *become her own mother.* She will be all she needs, self-sufficient, but – like the dead mother – she will be arrested in her capacity to love. Green says of the child's frozen love: *This cold core burns like ice, and numbs like it as well.* There will remain a gulf between the child and those she seeks to love, continuing into adulthood.

I had been an only child until I was seven when, much to my surprise, my sister was born. A few months earlier, my mother had asked me if I *would like a baby brother or sister?*

No, thanks, I had replied, imagining that would be the end of the matter. I didn't understand why she would think I might like a sibling. I had two parents, a cat, a doting grandmother nearby. I had a playroom and a garden. I had my friend Fiona across the street. What else did I need?

One day, though, I came home from school, delighted to find my mother back from the hospital. *Shhh!* she said. *You'll wake the baby!*

My baby sister's arrival changed everything. It would not be until we were grown up that my sister and I enjoyed each other's company or spent time together by choice.

And it was only through my sister that I learned – as an adult – that my mother had lost a second-trimester baby when I was about two years old, although I knew that she had suffered many miscarriages. In the twenty-first century, the birth could be registered, the baby could be named, a funeral held. Then, in the mid–1960s, my mother had to labour at home to give birth to a dead child. My grandmother (with whom my parents lived until I was three) was told by the attending doctor to *dispose of it.*

I have no memory of any of this, nor of what preceded it: my mother's pregnancy had been precarious for some time so she was prescribed total bed rest and instructed by her doctor not to pick me up. My maternal grandmother became my primary caregiver while my father was at work. So my mother was suddenly and inexplicably removed from close contact with me and then she was in mourning for her lost child, a son apparently. Who knows for how long, or what the ongoing impact of subsequent failed pregnancies had on her state of mind or our relationship?

The most common cause of the dead mother complex, Green believed, was one *which remains totally hidden, because the manifest signs by which the child could recognize it, and thus gain retrospective knowledge of it, is never possible because it rests on a secret: a miscarriage of the mother.*

⚥

All of which is a long way from Agnes in her dressing gown bringing me a morning coffee. But nonetheless there I was at the Retreat, simultaneously feeling both a blank emptiness and an overwhelming dread, almost giddy with such divergent reactions. I was uncharacteristically unable to articulate my thoughts or even to identify them as they skidded across my consciousness.

After another hour of fruitless conversation Agnes and I were at an impasse and we sat in silence. It was then that Agnes offered to drive me home and I grasped the opportunity like a lifeline. I'm not sure I've ever been happier than when I unloaded my bags from her car and waved Agnes goodbye from my driveway.

That first night home, though, I had an unsettling nightmare. I have always felt cheated when authors relate dreams in books. It's almost as bad as real people re-telling their dreams to you over breakfast. After all, authors can make up anything they like and describing dreams seems like a lazy substitute for better characterisation or plotting. If I was going to make something up, though, I would hope for something more subtle, but my unconscious did not really make much of an effort that night. A larger-than-life female figure – a goddess? – transformed from a towering presence of benevolence to violent avenger in an instant. My beloved whippet was murdered, split in half, and hung up like a carcass in a butcher's window. I woke up distraught, overcome with relief that the dog was still snoring beside me. But I didn't sleep again that night.

The next day, as the dream lingered unpleasantly, I suddenly remembered a recurring dream I had through childhood, starting at the age of three or four, when my family had moved to live directly across the road from my grandmother. In the two years we lived there, I dreamed *the green witch dream* regularly and it persisted intermittently through my childhood, even occasionally into adolescence. In this dream, there was a gigantic green witch standing in the middle of the street between my grandmother's house and my house, towering over the neighbourhood. I was terrified she was going to break into our house and kill us all, starting with my parents, whose room, across the hallway from mine, faced onto the street. Only as the dream continued, however, did I become aware that the green witch's presence in the middle of the road meant that she had already killed my grandmother and that was why she was now turning her attention to our house, and I would wake up, devastated and weeping.

19.

And
you're
there

Despite my nightmare, in the days after I returned from the Retreat I felt like Jimmy Stewart at the end of *It's a Wonderful Life*, running exuberantly around his neighbourhood, reclaiming his life. Instead of retreat I felt as though I had advanced, progressing to a new stage where I could start to gain some real distance from the dark days and contemplate the future again. It was as if something had definitively shifted, as *if the doors of my heart* had opened by a chink. *Every morning, so far, I'm alive*, I reminded myself. The question of what to do next, however, remained.

Yoga often seems to plays a role in the recovery phase of depression memoirs but I had never had the slightest interest in it. Like Matt Haig in his depression memoir, I would have described myself as a *yogaphobe* even though, in recovery from my second breakdown during my early 30s, I had meditated at home every morning and found it a calming practice. I had also flirted with Buddhism then, reading everything by Pema Chödrön I could find

and attending day-long meditation retreats. In a room with 50 other
people meditating in a Fremantle ashram on a hot summer's day,
an hour would fly by like minutes and afterwards I would feel both
refreshed and reinvigorated. But the tiered ranks of gods on the mural
at the front of the meditation room made me uneasy; I was in the
process of cutting my ties to the faith in which I had been raised and
was in no hurry to commit to another one. I soon stopped attending
retreats and eventually dropped my daily meditation practice, too,
thinking I didn't need it any more.

My sole experience of a yoga class was also in Perth, where a
no-nonsense friend who did not strike me as the yoga type assured
me that the class she attended was *not like normal yoga* so, on her
recommendation, I gave it a try. Five minutes into the class I was so
cross I could have screamed. I was embarrassingly inflexible, unable to
achieve what seemed like the simplest poses. The stifling community
hall was packed with people and the teacher seemed far away, issuing
clipped instructions with little elaboration or encouragement, hard
to see through the crowd. The other pupils seemed unfazed by the
atmosphere, not on the verge of tears like me. And then, after 50
minutes of boot-camp yoga, the mode of the class suddenly shifted. We
were all supposed to lie quietly on our mats and meditate. I lay there
seething and breathing shallowly to avoid being overcome by the acrid
smell of body odour that now permeated the hall.

That first summer in Matakana, however, I surprised myself by
thinking *I'd like to take up yoga*. I suppose it was part of my fantasy
about the new, serene way of life I was going to pursue – growing
vegetables, baking bread, raising goats. I would become a self-possessed
and supple practitioner of yoga and meet other like-minded women in
the area. A kind of *Ladies of the Canyon* fantasy.

My husband had the vegetable growing well in hand and the goats
were largely self-sufficient so I went back to baking, as I used to do
before the dark times. Rosemary focaccia, coconut loaf, lemon cake,
cinnamon swirls.

That just left yoga. There was a sign outside the village hall for
a weekly beginners' yoga class but I had been hoping for a more
congenial venue, probably because I spent too many years in my
youth in dusty and draughty halls enduring weekly sessions of
Physical Culture – or *Physsie* (pronounced 'fizzy') – a bizarre blend of

callisthenics and ballet popular in Australia in the 1960s and 70s that featured uniforms and makeup with all the subtlety of kiddy beauty pageants.

I googled a few other possibilities in the area, including a yoga studio in the valley directly below the ridge where we lived. So I turned up there one Friday morning, fearing public humiliation but thinking *I'll just try it once*, after the teacher had assured me by email that this class was small and low-key.

Sally's white-walled and timber-framed studio was in a sheltered corner of the valley surrounded by her flourishing garden. Tomatoes, courgettes, aubergines, lettuce. Scarlet runner beans climbing up bamboo tepees. Pumpkin vines twining along the edge of the bed. Strawberries with the promise of fruit to come and sunflowers towering over all. Citrus trees laden with ripening fruit. Inside the airy studio the windows were thrown open so that their white gauze curtains lifted in the breeze.

That first 90-minute class was both soothing and absorbing. In a state of intense concentration, I tried to direct my body to the poses and by the end of the class realised I had not had a single opportunity for self-reviling. Even though my abilities were extremely limited, Sally was calm and encouraging and the other pupils – women around my own age, all experienced regulars – were cheerful and welcoming. I felt no judgement. I had no expectations, did not hold myself to a high standard of success. I was just curious to try to follow the instructions which urged me to move and think in an utterly unfamiliar way. I don't recall ever enjoying failure so much or being content simply to try.

I was hooked by that first class and even as I unravelled into relapse I still kept up my classes. Yoga was like a time-out from depression. Somehow, I could usually bracket off that 90 minutes in the morning from the obsessive misery that was reasserting its presence during the remainder of the day. There was only one class when I was close to tears, where the movements and the need to pay attention to my body unexpectedly triggered a strong flood of sadness. Sally noticed. I toyed with the idea of running from the studio to my car but I stayed, held the pose, breathed, brushed away a tear, and made it to the end of class. But I spent the rest of that day in bed.

After I returned from the Retreat, or the Reprieve as I started to call it, I continued to attend yoga twice a week without fail. I started to feel a slow improvement – very slow – even though no two classes followed exactly the same sequence of poses so that the sessions were never routine or predictable. Encouraged by the soothing presence of Sally, I resisted any self-imposed pressure to progress more quickly. I kept my eyes on my mat and did my own work. Sally would notice the slightest improvement when any of us had struggled to achieve a position. Sometimes she would put out a guiding hand to make an adjustment to your pose and say quietly, *And you're there. Can you feel that?*

And I could.

The yoga studio was such a quiet space that occasionally during the *savasana*, the relaxation pose that ended every class, I would be distracted, not by the chatter of my own interior monologue (for once), but by the birdsong outside in the garden. *I'm sure that was a kingfisher.* And then I would lose the breath, trying to imagine where the bird was calling from and whether it was alone or was there a nest nearby? Then there might be the distinctive trill of a riroriro and I could not block that out either. I had to tune in to its cadence, wait for it to call again. *Wait – what's happened to my breath again?*

Within the gentle practice of Sally's studio, though, I began to be able to confront imperfection, failure, on a small scale, with the lowest of stakes. There would be no blame if I failed. No shame. And I still left the class feeling looser, lighter, alert, relaxed, even if I had wobbled and hunched my way through every pose, with crooked arms and bent legs.

Everything I had read about my illness and the so-called survival strategies that had accreted around it – defence mechanisms that fed into the deluded thinking of phobia – had convinced me of the futility of my pitched battle between mind and body, but until I began yoga I had no effective way to end a fight I was always losing. To show fear, to fail, to be weak, was so shaming, so unbearable, that it must be concealed at all costs. The obsessive thoughts that led me to avoid contact with anything potentially contaminating were a doomed attempt to put all the shit elsewhere, away from me, to keep myself above all the unpleasantness of life, the world, the body. Being constantly fearful but wanting, needing, to be self-sufficient, under control, *in* control, was an everyday contradiction for me that was unsustainable, and exhausting.

I was now starting to understand the symptoms associated with phobia (avoidance, panic, OCD) as the body's attempt to respond to ideas, memories, feelings that I wanted to push away, forget, block out, disown. Desperately trying to reject and expel the badness from inside had meant always trying to be vigilant for retaliation from an imperfect world outside. But the paradox is that it is only by acknowledging, by tolerating the badness *inside* that you can begin to relinquish fear. Up until now, I had only been able to understand my body as a source of betrayal through its potential for contamination and its panicked response to exposure, so that it had become the enemy – or *the persecutor*, in Winnicott's terms. It was not simply the world that was the enemy but my body, myself. That's why I was always doomed to fail in my attempts to overcome the enemy, trying to make myself invulnerable to contact or contamination. The boundary could never be impermeable, that's what being alive means.

Even something as minor as standing barefoot in yoga class, spreading my toes, feeling full contact with the floor through the soles of my feet, took me into a different sense of the body and what it means to inhabit one, to be bodily. I can't achieve the poses the way that I would like to but, even as a beginner, I felt less like my body is the enemy. We are in this together, mind and body, breath and matter, stillness and movement. I (whoever that is) am more forgiving of its – my – failures.

I don't claim to know anything about yoga beyond my own limited experience. I have not researched yoga practice. I don't see it as a spiritual exercise. But I had stumbled on a process that seemed to go to the heart of my symptoms and their underlying causes and start to heal them. The quietness of yoga practice was able to still my mind and its yabbering recriminations. The focus on connecting body and mind through the breath, thinking into the body as it were, chipped away at my sense of alienation from the body. I have a different sense of embodiment than I used to, an awareness of how I stand, how I am aligned, how I breathe, that is fundamentally different to the hypersensitivity that I experienced in episodes of phobic-OCD symptoms.

I have always had a low boredom threshold. Regular exercise of any kind is a constant challenge not simply because I am lazy but because it is mostly dull and repetitive. Walking or running outdoors offer the diversions of a changing landscape but even that can feel like a chore. A yoga class, by contrast, holds my attention throughout. It requires concentration but does not leave me feeling drained like other activities that demand a high degree of focus. I hate to use the word but I guess it is *mindful*. It is equally bodyful.

Sally's studio had become a kind of holding environment for me – an environment that encourages a *going-on-being*, a term coined by Winnicott that resonates with me. (So often, Winnicott seemed to come up with inelegant terms for something important, something we lack a single word to capture well, but a word that stops us in our tracks.) *Going-on-being* is what we hope to do as humans – not just to survive but to thrive in the unpredictable and uncontrollable conditions that we encounter. As humans, Winnicott thought, we develop and grow through experimenting with life – with *play*, actually, to use his preferred term – *finding through pleasure what interests us*. That's how we learn. *Going-on-being* is therefore fundamentally a creative process, and it is always transitional, inconclusive. A *holding environment* – beyond the nurture of infancy – is one where we feel safe to do all this: to be creative, to try, to enjoy, to play, to fail, to learn. Without such environments, we wither and die.

I often think that an observer could walk past the windows during our yoga class and think there was not much going on. A small group of women (mostly), not doing anything particularly beautiful or dramatic with their bodies – standing, sitting, lying, stretching, bending. It would be boring to watch. Okay, sometimes we hang upside-down from rope harnesses but that is as exciting as it gets. Nothing much to see. But so much happening.

20.

Think of the long trip home

At this point in my recovery, my father Skyped from Australia one morning. He was sobbing, so it was difficult for him to speak, but he told me that my mother had just been diagnosed with motor neurone disease, a terminal condition with a short life expectancy. What had started as a sense of lameness, numbness, in her lower left leg, and had been resistant to any physiotherapy, had resulted in a referral to a neurologist – some months ago, my father revealed. He and my mother had resigned themselves to the public-health waiting list and, in the meantime, they had adjusted to Mum's limited mobility: a walking stick, a power-assisted armchair. They already lived a quiet, sedentary life on the Central Coast of New South Wales. My mother didn't drive so they typically went everywhere together – shopping, doctors' appointments, church groups – and, initially, little had changed for them. With a confirmed diagnosis, however, it became clear that they had both been refusing to contemplate what my mother's lameness could signify. My mother always seemed to have a string of relatively minor health complaints so I could imagine how they might have chosen to see this as just another ailment that could eventually be remedied by the right prescription or, at worst, minor surgery. This news, then, shook them both hard.

I, too, was shaken: my father's uncharacteristic tears underlined the seriousness of his revelation. My mother, by contrast, seemed more resigned to the news. I will never know now how much she had really suspected all along about her condition. When my father carried the laptop to my mother's bedroom so I could speak to her, she was subdued but more under control than my father. I had a million questions – what *exactly* did the doctor say? What happened next? What could be done? – but I couldn't yet begin to feel (or allow myself to feel) anything. I ended the call promising to come and visit soon. Dad cried some more; Mum seemed pleased at the idea of my visit.

After speaking to my parents, I phoned my sister, K, in Sydney; she had also just received the news, although she told me that she had always feared the matter was more serious than my parents were prepared to acknowledge. She had been to visit them and had observed how my mother's leg seemed to be withering, shrunk to half the size of her other leg as the disused muscles contracted. K had encouraged my parents to see if the neurologist's appointment could be brought forward. They had preferred to wait for fate to take its course.

Over the years, K and I had shared many conversations where we compared notes on our parents. Such was the closeness of our parents (despite their eternal bickering) that they had seemed to construct a world-for-two (the uncharitable might describe it as a *folie à deux*) that sometimes bore little resemblance to the everyday reality the rest of us inhabited. So K and I – divided by distance as I moved from place to place, country to country, while she remained in inner-city Sydney – often discovered, during our long-distance calls, that we had each been told wildly different versions of the same event, to suit our parents' perception of which daughter would be less likely to criticise their latest hare-brained scheme. *You won't believe what they're planning now,* one sister would tell the other.

After my father took early retirement from the ministry, my parents had continued their peripatetic ways – moving to Perth for a few years (while I was living there) before heading back east, first to the north coast of New South Wales (back to my father's home town), then to the south coast (again) – before settling on the Central Coast, although 'settling' was always a very relative term for them. Despite advancing years and depleted financial resources, they had continued to move from house to house in and around the Central Coast.

I had another month or so left in New Zealand – allowing time for a short trip across the Tasman. I hoped my improved OCD could handle travel to an unfamiliar place (not having visited my parents since their most recent move) and I asked my sister if she wanted to come with me, if she would be able to free herself of family obligations for a few days. I would welcome her company on what I knew would be a difficult journey and she had a closer relationship with my mother than I ever had. My daughter, M, wanted to come along too, when she learned the news of her grandmother's illness, and managed to rearrange her work schedule. So M and I flew from Auckland to Sydney, collected a hire car and my sister, and the three of us set off on an unlikely road trip that none of us could have envisaged even a couple of weeks previously.

Driving north from Sydney up the Pacific Highway, everything was deeply familiar and slightly disorienting, as it always is whenever I return to Australia now. This road, in particular, was one I had travelled countless times since infancy, and landmarks like the Mooney Mooney bridge brought more than a tinge of nostalgic recognition. But the road north was now a multi-lane highway, instead of a mostly winding narrow thoroughfare where overtaking had been a life-threatening activity.

For my daughter, the coast of New South Wales was a largely new experience. Her years in New Zealand were dimming her memories of the Australian landscape and she had developed a Kiwi aversion to its dangers. The novelty of the wildlife, however, had its compensations. During this visit, one of the things we would do to ease the tension associated with visiting a dying mother/grandmother was drive around in the late afternoon looking for mobs of kangaroos sitting by the side of the road or on golf-course fairways. Dusk is a good time for roo-spotting as they tend to graze more openly then, away from the cover of the bush. *There they are*, my sister would say from the back seat, bemused by our excitement at what was nothing remarkable for her, just a few roos, and I would pull over so M could jump out of the car for a photo.

When we arrived on the first day of our visit, the sight of my mother's decline – she had become a little, frail old woman – momentarily took the air from my chest and I saw my sense of shock reflected on M's face too. Mum had made an effort to dress well and apply makeup in a way that touched even my cold heart, and she hobbled with her stick to the front door to greet us, even though we told her not to. Behind her, my father was remonstrating: *Listen to the girls! Sit down! Sit down! You don't have to do that! Stay in your chair; they'll come to you.*

My parents' house smelled bad. Nothing was clean. My mother had always been an exemplary housekeeper but things had clearly slipped now that she was mostly confined to bed or armchair. The carpet was crunchy underfoot. A mélange of items was jumbled on the side table between my parents' two armchairs – old computer cables, pens, a coloured pencil or two, junk mail, a bottle cap, a packet of pills. Craft projects that Mum would never be able to complete now that her fine motor skills had started to deteriorate were left wherever she had last worked on them around the house.

Dad did all the cooking now so Mum probably never entered the kitchen any more. She wouldn't have seen how not a single surface was clear of food scraps or unwiped spills. The contents of the fridge were a horror to behold and betrayed the source of the smell. The dishwasher was broken and all the cups and glasses were sticky and smeary, if not stained. K and I took it in turns to make cups of tea but I brought my own bottle of water, ate nothing, touched as little as possible. I was too cowardly to face cleaning up the mess. A trip to the bathroom was an ordeal. M and I used hand sanitiser frequently; K was made of tougher stuff and took it in her stride. She had known what to expect, having braved previous visits.

Most of the time with my parents we spent reminiscing, looking at old family photos, trying to avoid any contentious topics or the reason that had brought the three of us here. There were many retellings of

well-worn family anecdotes. Dad enjoyed relating these stories and
we indulged him. We knew them all so well, even the untrue bits, not
quite how things happened but how they had been told, over and
over. My mother laughed a lot and chipped in with some of her own
stories. She and M sat close together.

There were, though, uncomfortable pauses and times when
someone would get up to leave the room so they could brush away
a tear, unnoticed. Then we would persuade my parents to come out
with us in the afternoon – to lunch at a restaurant on the bay, or for
a drive through the bush. My father would grumble and think of
reasons why we should stay put but my mother was keen to leave
the house; she didn't want to miss any opportunity for an outing. I
fell into my organising-eldest-child mode, keeping up the excessive
politeness that had become my default mode as an adult whenever
I visited my parents, avoiding being left alone with my mother, and
doing my best to feel nothing at all.

By mid-afternoon, back at their house, we would make our
excuses and leave: *You two need a rest*, we would say. And it was true,
both my parents would be exhausted by then and in need of a nap;
even they would admit it. *We'll see you again tomorrow*, we'd say, as both
my parents shed tears. Each day, as soon as we left their house, we
would make a stop at the local bottle shop for supplies.

We stayed three days; it felt like a month. I had found a
comfortable B&B by the water about 20 minutes from my parents',
and in the evenings, back at the B&B, I would drink too much (free of
my parents' disapproval as lifelong teetotallers). After dinner, the three
of us would sit outside with our drinks, raw from the emotion of the
day, and watch the evening close in over the inlet framed by dense
bush down to the shoreline. I was so grateful to have my daughter and
my sister with me so we could say whatever we wanted to each other,
talk complete nonsense, or say nothing at all.

When M and I flew back to New Zealand, I felt like I could
breathe again. My mother's prognosis was uncertain – *it could be years
before she declined any further*, my father told me, and I chose to believe
him. I promised to come back soon.

☙

But first I needed to return to England, my period of research leave over. I dreaded leaving New Zealand again, leaving behind my family. Leaving my dog and the goats. Leaving the birds and the bush and the beach. It did not seem possible that I would board a plane and suddenly not be there. I planned to return to them all during the university's summer break, when Matakana would be in the depths of its wet winter, but it was difficult, in the final two weeks at home, not to feel an oppressive dread as departure day inevitably approached. The season was visibly turning – more colour on the trees, the full extent of European flora now evident in a way that the lush greens of summer had disguised – and the arrival of autumn marked the end of my stay.

After the long flight back to Heathrow, jet lag hit me harder than usual. I returned to a full desk at work and a new term. Without family responsibilities, I could be in the office before eight and stay till six, but I was waking at four in the morning when the sky began to lighten and dropping into bed by 8pm, drinking too much coffee and still feeling slightly groggy much of the day. I was going through the motions, returning to a world where people welcomed me back warmly, as if I belonged there, but being back on campus felt surreal and disembodied.

It was a shock, then, once the jet lag subsided and I was establishing a routine again – running in the morning, working during the day, knitting in the evening – to have a sudden awareness that the last vestiges of the dark, dead weight of depression had evaporated. A lot of the time I could block out thinking about my mother's illness, although I Skyped my parents regularly; things seemed much the same as when I visited. My father was collecting stories – from the GP, from the internet – of *people who had lived for years with MND without noticeable decline*, so I allowed myself to believe them too.

I was still wrestling with a final decision about how and when to leave my job in England, still facing at least another six months of living a life split between two sides of the world. But all of that was different, engaged a different part of my mind, from the deadening thoughts of depression and the blankness of my default response under its influence.

One morning I was standing in the kitchen of my cottage in Sandwich watching the starlings bicker on the next door's bird feeder, just visible over the stone wall between our houses, when I realised *I'm not depressed any more.* It was just over a week since I had returned to England to find the town dotted with wisteria and lilacs in the full bloom of a late spring. The lanes were filled with sweet fragrance; around every corner, it seemed, bursts of purple, mauve or white draped from walls or waved above them. I heard a cuckoo, calling from the same tree, every morning on my run.

I had no way of accounting for it, this sense that the *unaliveness* had finally passed (for now? how long?). I still did not feel at home in England but it was as if I had made my peace with being here. The sense of my home in Matakana as an anchor that now grounded and aligned me, wherever I was on the earth's surface, somehow gave me a new resilience when the daily irritations with English life arose.

My OCD symptoms had also alleviated. Sometimes I actually forgot to use hand sanitiser. I still scanned people's faces for signs of illness, still avoided door handles and performed most of the other rituals I hoped would ward off contamination. I still hated shaking hands with people but I didn't have the same sense that I was bracing myself against an encounter with a deeply hostile world every time I left the house.

21.

Morning over Sussex

My small black car beetled along among a string of white vans. I had set a route on the satnav to avoid motorways, so I was driving a cross-country hypotenuse from Sandwich to Lewes on A and B roads. A grey chill hugged the East Kent coast when I set out but as I drove inland the temperature slowly climbed and a blue sky emerged. By the time I stepped out of the car in Sussex it was a perfect summer's day. The warm appeal of a Sussex summer even began to temper my wish to leave England behind forever. *Think of the winters*, I reminded myself.

The further southwest I travelled, the more *Vote Leave* signs sprang up by the side of the road, mostly in people's front gardens. It was two weeks before the Brexit referendum. The depressing reminders of little England's fervent desire to pull up the drawbridge – which, to everyone's surprise, would be satisfied – were lightened only by a vicar's attempt at relevance, on a sign outside a village church: *Kingdom of God, In or Out?*

In a sense, I have already voted to leave, despite the fact that I am still here. I am back in Britain for the teaching term but my stay feels temporary, provisional. I have an escape plan ready to activate whenever I feel the need. No protracted negotiations necessary, just a quick resignation. All it would take is a final decision on my part. But I am not quite there yet; I will see how the next term goes.

The garish *Take back control of our country* signs were a sombre note in what would otherwise have been southeast England at its best – black-faced sheep in impossibly green fields, prosperous white-timbered villages and, eventually, the South Downs appearing over the surrounding landscape, *soaring, like birds' wings sweeping up & up,* as Virginia Woolf observed over 70 years ago, on the brink of a far more catastrophic rupture with Europe.

Approaching Lewes, different signs began to appear, quite frequently. *JOY,* they read. After the first couple of these took my attention, I noticed the smaller print below: it was, apparently, *A boutique summer festival of music, food & drink, homeware, in the heart of lovely Lewes.* So I'm on a journey to a place my family once called home (my grandparents had emigrated from Lewes), where joy can be found. I swear if this wasn't true I would have come up with something less clichéd.

ᴡ

The Scandi-blanc therapist I had visited at the start of the downward spiral had summarised my first session with her: *You want to regain some joy in your life.*

But did I want joy in my life? Joy was already in my life, as noted earlier, as a middle name I have always hated, even more than I dislike my first name, which has all the gravitas of a kitten without any of the heart-melting cuteness. *Wendy* – a name from a children's book about a boy who never grows up, given to a girl who happily takes on the care of other motherless boys.

By contrast, *Joy* at least seemed an unremarkable name, insignificant, just a place-holder middle name, a monosyllabic afterthought. Or so I thought until, somewhere around that threshold between late childhood and early adolescence, I overheard my mother explaining to a friend one day why she liked the name and had given it to me.

I've always liked the Christian meaning of the word, my mother said. *You know? The initials stand for Jesus first, others second, yourself last –* J.O.Y.

Yourself last. It was there in my name – an imperative not to put myself forward, to be significant, to matter. What is a child supposed to do with that information? Whatever the word may have meant to a devout parent bestowing the name, what can a child hear except self-negation?

So the word 'joy' has always made me twitchy. I avoid using it, which is challenging because it has such a resonant history in literature; the Romantic poets, in particular, loved *the deep power of joy.* But what to use instead? 'Bliss' sounds a bit too hippy-dippy (as in *Follow your bliss*). 'Rapture' is a word favoured by Virginia Woolf, but for those raised in fundamentalist doctrines it is beyond reclaim. (I recall reading some freaky Christian comics in the 1970s about the Rapture, showing bodies floating up into the sky, cars without drivers suddenly crashing off bridges, empty desks in schools and offices, while those left behind looked bereft and terrified.) What else, then? Euphoria? Ecstasy? Too grandiose, overblown, psychotropic even. There is a simplicity to 'joy' that lends itself equally to the extraordinary or the everyday. I get that. But I just can't use it. It always sounds like death to me. (And as I write that word *death,* pushing away the thought that all this time my mother is dying slowly, not knowing when each vital function will cease to be possible unaided – walking, eating, breathing.)

When I arrived at Monk's House after stopping for lunch in Lewes, I didn't actually notice it. Following the signs to the carpark a little beyond the house must inevitably mean that many drivers – like me – miss the unassuming white-timbered exterior fronting the road, just one among many similar village houses. Having parked, I approached the house on foot, unlatching the garden gate and walking around to the back of the house alone. The other visitors were either already inside or scattered out of sight through the garden so I momentarily felt I had the place to myself, or was an invited guest. But then the smiling National Trust guide appeared at the door, directing me to the ground-floor sitting room while beginning her spiel: *Monk's House was the Woolfs' country home, a chance to get away from London and relax ...*

I smiled and nodded and kept walking. The sitting room was occupied by another NT guide and two older women, admiring the painting by the fireplace of the Woolfs' dog. The room was modestly furnished. Armchairs by the hearth. A table and chairs colourfully painted by Vanessa Bell. Books, scattered and in small piles. The other rooms open to the public were also on the ground floor. The small dining room and part of the kitchen I passed through quickly. I was here to see Virginia's bedroom, beside the kitchen, requiring you to leave through the kitchen door as there is no direct access from the house.

I had seen photographs of the white-draped single bed against a wall of bookshelves, looking as virginal as a nun's cell. Standing in the room, though, dispelled this assumption. The bed sits beneath a large picture window that lets in garden views and – today – floods the room with warmth and light, aided by another smaller window next to the door. It is a garden room as much as a bedroom, painted in shades of green and white, the garden growing right up to the door where a climbing pink rose flowers profusely and frames the side window too. A restful space.

Or so it was, at least, on my second visit to the room. When I first entered Virginia's bedroom it felt uncomfortably full: six other visitors and a seated guide. I was uneasy, complicit with this invasion of a private space. Four of the visitors were Americans, discussing with the guide the sale of valuable first editions of Woolf's works to an American. *How much are they worth now?* they wondered. *How do the Brits feel about them being in American ownership?* The guide replied non-committally, diplomatically, but one of the other visitors (a Londoner, he said) joked: *Well, I guess we didn't give back the Elgin marbles, did we?* Everyone laughed.

I fled to the garden, down the brick path leading to the orchard where Virginia's writing studio was located, past a prolific white rose, purple irises, a flesh-coloured clematis covering a wall so thickly that the bricks were invisible behind its blooms. I stopped by a small square pond – one of several of various shapes and sizes scattered through the garden – with a yellow iris in one corner and a spread of pink waterlilies radiating across the surface from another. Under a blush magnolia by the pond was a sculptured bust of Virginia, marking the spot where her ashes were scattered.

There's an age limit to leggings, said a man the wrong side of middle age, sitting on a white garden bench at the farthest point of the pond away from where I was standing under the magnolia.

Is there? said the younger woman sitting beside him. His daughter? An older woman – his wife? – who had been photographing the waterlilies rejoined the pair on the bench.

What's that? she said.

Ignoring his wife's question, the man persisted.

Yeah, 'cause there is, he said. *You don't want to see the way some women wear 'em, with the fat hangin' over the top, do you?*

The discussion continued – the daughter seeming to demur – but I moved on, eager to be out of earshot as soon as possible.

I was wearing leggings.

That's the problem, I find, with travelling alone. You imagine you are going to have a moment, be moved by an encounter with a place or landscape or artwork, experiencing to the full the impressions and feelings it evokes, without distraction. But what happens, of course, is *because* you are on your own you can't help but overhear other people's conversations, which seem terribly loud and obtrusive by contrast with your own silence.

Virginia Woolf's writing studio was against the far wall of the plot, with the village church directly behind it. Within Monk's House garden, the studio is flanked by the small orchard (with beehives) on one side and the expansive bowling green on the other. Beyond the green, the view extends to the chalk cliffs of the downs although the river is not visible. I had not expected to find such a vista opening out from a garden behind a house in the middle of the village. I sat on a deckchair in deep shade, directly outside the window that Virginia's writing desk faces. In front of me, a set of lawn bowls was scattered invitingly on the grass next to their wicker basket. A few other visitors were dotted across the expansive lawn, sitting on other deckchairs or on a bench by another pond, but for now, I was alone.

Let's try these out! The Americans reappeared and the two men each picked up a bowl. But they mistook them for boules and started tossing them across the green, each heavy ball landing with a thud.

Great shot, Dad! shouted the younger woman before wandering off towards the studio. The older American woman called after her, *What's in that little cabin, Molly?*

☙

At Monk's House, the house and grounds are contained; they are a world unto themselves. As Woolf wrote in her diary in 1932:

> Back from a good weekend at Rodmell – a weekend of no talking, sinking into deep safe book-reading; & then sleep: clear transparent; with the may tree like a breaking wave outside; & all the garden green tunnels, mounds of green; & then to wake into the hot still day, & never a person to be seen, never an interruption; the place to ourselves; the long hours.

It is not surprising that this quotation is on display at Monk's House. A beautiful weekend retreat, as packaged by the National Trust. Here is how they describe it on their website: *Nestled in the heart of rural Sussex, Monk's House is a tranquil 17th-century weatherboarded cottage inhabited by Leonard and the novelist Virginia Woolf from 1919 until Leonard's death in 1969.* Where is Virginia's death? She disappears somewhere between the *1919* and *Leonard's death*. She has no death recorded, as if she too somehow inhabited the house until 1969. Her suicide cannot be named, let alone the significance of Monk's House in that event.

There is nothing to suggest the close connection between the house and the river. You have no sense of it from the garden. There are no signposts indicating its proximity or how to get there. I wondered how many visitors asked the guides for directions. When I asked the smiling woman at the front door she replied without missing a beat (still smiling), *You go back to the car park, turn right, and keep walking. It takes about twenty minutes.*

Her pat response indicated I am clearly not the first to ask her this question. I did not elaborate as to why I might be interested to know. She exhibited no curiosity.

I set off, according to her instructions, not sure why I was doing this. Was it ghoulish? Was it research? Or a pilgrimage? But I gave up after only a few minutes – I was approaching a farmhouse with barking dogs, and a horse van was blocking the lane. It was also a hot afternoon and my water bottle was now empty. And I was self-conscious: a woman in her 50s, looking to retrace Virginia's steps. How pretentious. How predictable.

So I went back to my car, having learned nothing except that one would have to set off purposefully to the river; it was not simply a beckoning presence at the bottom of the garden to which one could be drawn on an impulse, then or now.

❦

Monk's House speaks of life, creativity, fecundity. Virginia's light and sunny bedroom reflects and echoes the *green tunnels, mounds of green* outside. Her studio is framed by trees and the buzzing of bees. It is a place that makes you want to breathe, to write, to live. I don't know, can't know, if it would have struck me this same way if I had visited Monk's House when living held less appeal for me, because illness ruptures our experience and disrupts everything we take for granted.

In her essay 'On Being Ill', Woolf writes: *There is, let us confess it (and illness is the great confessional), a childish outspokenness in illness; things are said, truths blurted out, which the cautious respectability of health conceals.* To be ill is to speak like a child, to speak of childish things. It is to speak of things that adults don't speak of because the isolation of the invalid opens up a new form of perception. *Directly the bed is called for,* Woolf continues,

> we cease to be soldiers in the army of the upright; we become deserters. They march to battle. We float with the sticks on the stream; helter-skelter with the dead leaves on the lawn, irresponsible and disinterested and able, perhaps for the first time for years, to look round, to look up — to look, for example, at the sky.

Shaken out of our customary experience of the world and ourselves, we are *able* in some way that we are not when we are well. Able to see, to witness, to feel, and — Woolf hopes — to speak.

Throughout this essay, Woolf's primary example of illness was influenza — mentioned five times in the first three pages — the most common of illnesses (and one, of course, that had taken on a tragic scale after World War One, as Woolf's first readers in 1926 would have been painfully aware). Once, just once, does she mention melancholia as a comparable illness, but it seems to me that one of the things this essay skirts around, as it plays with the binary of confession/disclosure, is mental illness.

I wonder how a condition like motor neurone disease fits with this idea of illness as a source of revelation, confession, epiphany? The circumlocution in all my conversations with my parents now was as far from *childish outspokenness* as it was possible to be. Did my mother feel able *to look round, to look up*, spending all day in her armchair facing away from the window in her cluttered living room?

☙

Until I visited Monk's House I hadn't known that Woolf, like me, liked to sleep with the curtains open to keep the sky in sight at all times. In the sky Woolf saw not only immeasurable beauty but indifference to human suffering and finitude, which she found strangely comforting. I don't look at the sky so much now. Does that mean I am better? Or just busier, more distracted? I get my fill of sky but I do other things too, now.

Like this trip – an overnight stay to see somewhere I had never been before, as well as to revisit Lewes where, as a young girl, my grandmother had worked in the brewery and, on weekends, walked to Brighton and back, for fun. My first visit to Lewes had been with my parents on our family's first trip to England almost 30 years ago, when we had visited the church where my grandmother was married, the street where she lived.

The following morning I re-traced my drive across Sussex, back to Sandwich, paying less attention to the 'Leave' signs today. In 'Evening over Sussex: Reflections in a motor car', Woolf lamented her inability to convey

> what one saw now over Sussex so that another person could share it … for beauty spread at one's right hand, at one's left; at one's back too; it was escaping all the time; one could only offer a thimble to a torrent that could fill baths, lakes.

I was more impervious to beauty than I had been the day before, when the South Downs had shocked me with their presence, and when the novelty of an overnight trip (voluntarily deciding to stay

in a strange place, eat in an unfamiliar restaurant) had turned out
to be uneventful in the best possible way. I had set out for a Woolf
experience and had been moved by the blooms, the greens, the calm,
of the summer garden. I had seen her desk and stood in her bedroom.
It felt like a rite of recovery, the laying of a ghost perhaps, but then it
escaped me.

22.

Ephemeral streams

Once the summer term ended in England, I returned to Matakana in July for a couple of months, still prevaricating about my future. The unknowns that would open up if I resigned from my job presented concerns beyond the financial: I worried that too much time on my hands could unravel my recovery again; I worried that my mind would not accept voluntary resignation as a conscious choice but would re-label it as failure.

I lay in bed my first night at home listening to heavy winter rain fall on the roof, before succumbing to the sleep of oblivion that comes like a mercy when, after a long flight, the room has started to sway and you are not sure if your feet are yet on the ground. Next morning the sun returned (briefly) and I stepped out onto the verandah to re-familiarise myself with the view. I could hear the rushing of water – ephemeral streams that are triggered by rain, hidden from sight deep in the bushland fringing our paddocks, running down the slope of the hill to feed a tributary of the river in the valley below. These streams are the reason why our bushland remains damp and fertile all year round, allowing native ferns to flourish and providing a habitat for creatures like kōura (freshwater crayfish) and giant dragonflies. I had never heard the water run so loudly before.

Like other crustaceans, kōura are encased in a hard shell-like skin that eventually becomes too small for the growing creature and must be shed so they can continue to grow. In times of drought, they burrow down into the mud, or even between stones, to survive until the water returns. In a similar way, I suppose I had spent much of the past year trying to protect myself, closing in on myself to present as small a target to a predatory world as possible, and waiting for life, like flowing fresh water, to return.

As usual, it took a few days before my head felt like it had caught up with my body on this side of the world, and for both to come to terms with the abrupt change of season. In southeast England the days were at their longest and summer had been tentatively beginning when I left; I had worn sandals and summer dresses in the last week there. Here, my body resisted the short days and the sudden drop in temperature – the relative mildness of a North Island winter offset by the lack of central heating to which I had become accustomed in England. I rummaged resentfully through drawers looking for sweaters and thick socks, forgetting their whereabouts, unsure what country they were in now my possessions were divided between two countries.

I noticed with fresh eyes the changes that the winter had brought to the landscape. There was a greater openness to the prospect as the European trees were now bare of foliage; I hadn't realised there were so many deciduous exotic trees in the view from our house until winter stripped their leaves. Outlines were sharper, lacking the soft fullness that comes with the exuberant growth of the summer foliage. A house over the ridge that had been invisible all summer was now revealed through a gap in the bushline. Our kitchen garden bed was cleared, the summer vegetables all gone, only the bright red and yellow stalks of the Swiss chard and the flourishing rosemary bush undaunted by the change of season. But white arum lilies dotted across the paddocks in clumps were blooming abundantly, and the camellia bushes by the path to the garage were studded with crimson blooms like rosettes.

The two Orpington hens, Peggy and Fluffy, were bigger and rounder than ever, although their snowy white feathers were now speckled with the mud of the chicken yard; their three New Hampshire sisters, the Pankhursts – smaller and feistier – looked dowdy by comparison, their damp, tawny-red feathers lacking the gloss they had had in the summertime. At feeding time in the chicken yard, a rabble of sparrows descended, eager to share the poultry pellets and kitchen scraps. Rabbits, too, came in to feed, boldly sitting *in* the chicken feeder while hens pecked nonchalantly beside them. Some mornings it was like a scene from a Disney cartoon down there – rabbits and chickens side by side, flocks of sparrows sweeping in to land and hop about among the larger birds, while goats looked in from the other side of the fence, watching the show and awaiting their own breakfast delivery.

Changes in the wild bird life were also evident. Pīwakawaka, less visible in the summer, were now everywhere and never still – hovering around all the trees and shrubs in the garden, dancing on the lawn to display their fan tails, accompanying me and the dog on our daily walks (apparently because larger creatures like us are more likely to flush out the insects which the birds feed on, as we disturb the grass or brush against branches). One day, when a rare sunny afternoon made a walk along the beach possible, a pīwakawaka circled and darted around me as I walked from the carpark to the sand, as if keen for company or an audience for its energetic twisting and turning in flight, while it called with its distinctive chattering, 'kissing' sound: *cheek-cheek-cheek*. Kingfishers could still be seen here and there, both on the hills and in the valley, and the hawks regularly flew by our house on their rounds. The tūī were largely absent although occasionally they could be heard clicking and whistling in the undergrowth. And our resident morepork was still around – seen in silhouette on a branch of the tree just outside my bedroom window one evening, and hooting from further afield during the hours of darkness.

I didn't easily slip back into the routines I had established over the summer and early autumn in Matakana; the seasonal change had thrown me off-kilter, as had the need to readjust to a quieter, slower mode of life after the busyness of term time. In England, and free of depression, I had become much more sociable during the short summer term, regularly meeting with colleagues for drinks or dinner, and travelling to catch up with more distant friends I had not been able to see while my illness had kept me a virtual prisoner. I was able to talk more freely now about what I had been through, and was touched by the care and affection that others articulated for me, hearing in turn their own stories of struggle and sadness. At the invitation of a friend at another university, I had spoken at a symposium that sought to bridge the divide between feeling and thinking, between intellect and creativity, between illness and health, and for the first time I articulated in public some of what I have written here. That day I felt a possibility stirring, that *maybe* I could integrate the two parts of my life – the academic and the creative – rather than being forced to choose between them.

On that same day, though, I had struggled with familiar symptoms: in the stylish boutique hotel where I was staying, the spotless bathroom had smelled *too* strongly of bleach, causing me to fear that something dreadful had happened in there to warrant such a thorough cleaning. I tried hard to dispel the rising panic that I felt but I still spent the least time possible in the bathroom during my stay.

Now, back in Matakana for the southern winter, I found myself aimless. I couldn't settle to anything except watching the birds, walking the dog, feeding the goats and going to yoga. I loved all these things but I was forced to confront the possibility that what I had craved during my depression was not enough for a life post-recovery. Mark Rice-Oxley's words, *You tell yourself, if I recover I promise I will not want so much … It will be enough for me just to be myself again* – the internal bargaining of those hanging on to life by a thread – started to seem like something that I needed to cast off as too confining, too small.

I knew that I no longer wanted to have my life consumed by ambition and the relentless workload that had gone along with it. After all, what had ambition done for me, other than make me ill? But was I ready to relinquish my career entirely? Now, how could I best sustain my *going-on-being*? Was it possible to refashion a working life – a life of meaningful work – that was more creative, neither driven by overreaching and fear of failure, nor withdrawing entirely from a wider world? The geographical gulf between my career in one country and my home in another, 12 time zones away, was a fitting symbol for how divided and torn I felt between what seemed like two distinct ways of living and being in the world. Would such a split existence only perpetuate a divided self? Or would it allow me to have my cake and eat it too?

w

One afternoon – my son and husband absent at school and work – I dug out a recipe pasted into a saggy-spined book I had started to collate when I was first married. Its pages chart our changing tastes and food fads over the 30-plus years since then, as well as my evolving handwriting, gradually becoming less youthfully rounded, more an impatient scrawl. I had written one recipe on the back of a dot-matrix-printed bill from my first obstetrician, a marvellous woman who had arrived in the delivery room in a silk suit and a long string of pearls, and jollied my husband and me – equally terrified at the enormity of what was about to happen – through the birth of our daughter as if it was an entirely normal, everyday event. Other recipes were written on the backs of envelopes or torn from the *West Australian*, now yellowed as if from a past century, as indeed they were.

I wanted to make use of our surfeit of lemons but my usual lemon recipes didn't appeal so I had resorted to my oldest recipe book. Lemon Cheese Slice was written in my mother's distinctive and beautiful copperplate hand, one of many recipes she had written out for me over the years, most of them for traditional baking in which margarine features prominently. I marvelled again at my mother's handwriting, unchanged from her school years, each flourish uniform in shape and placement, the words perfectly spaced across a page torn roughly from a cheap notepad. No abbreviations or shortcuts in the instructions, just the occasional aside – (*pour quickly as it sets fast!*) – to suggest that the writer was experienced with the vagaries of this slice. I don't recall requesting this recipe, and certainly others in my book in her handwriting, like Lemon Mint Zinger, she had pressed on me unasked, imagining I might have an occasion when a pitcher of mint leaves, lemon slices, soda water, a bottle of lemonade and a few drops of green food colouring would be called for.

I mixed flour, sugar and unsalted butter in the food processor with a drizzle of cold water to make a pastry dough, pressed it out into a tin and pricked the base with a fork before baking it in the oven. While it cooked, I made the first lemon layer to go on top: lemon juice, sugar, water and custard powder in a saucepan stirred over heat until boiling and thick, then poured over the now-ready pastry base. Then the next layer, again made in a saucepan: milk, sugar, vanilla and a cornflour paste to make a thick and creamy topping to cover the transparent, viscous lemon layer. A dusting of desiccated coconut and then left to chill and set firm in the fridge.

No cheese of any kind in fact appears in Lemon Cheese Slice.

I don't think I had made that recipe since my daughter, now in her mid-20s, was small. Certainly my son, 10 years younger than his sister, has no recollection of Lemon Cheese Slice and remarked on its odd texture and appearance, but still ate it with the gusto of a ravenous 16-year-old when he came home from school. It wasn't heritage cooking worthy of the *Observer Monthly Food Magazine*, it was stodgy unfashionable fare from a time when the regular church-fellowship teas my family attended featured any number of similar confections. As a child, I would bypass the tinned asparagus spears wrapped in squares of white, crustless bread skewered by a toothpick, the slices of luncheon meat wrapped around cold lumps of mashed potato (again with the mandatory toothpick), and the three different kinds of chicken casserole (the yellow, the orange and the brown) in favour of the dessert table laden with slices and trifles to satisfy even my sweet tooth.

This wasn't usually a part of my past I was keen to revisit, but ever since the Retreat had conjured up the 'blank' child of those years, a wealth of memories had increasingly come to mind. Lemon Cheese Slice reminded me that I didn't have to scan every memory for signs of damage or unkindness. Sometimes there was comfort (food) too. What might it mean to recall more of that time without judgement – of the past, my parents, myself?

᭟

I thought of that cliché, *spreading yourself too thinly*. Was that what I was doing, by trying to live two lives on different sides of the world? Was it better for the self to pool, like a reservoir, to be deep rather than wide, or would that simply be to congeal? Does a spread self become too extensive, its surface tension stretched beyond breaking point? Leaving what? Globs of self, uncohered, disparate, cut off from each other? A stagnant series of puddles, without flow or connection?

Marion Milner had thought that *This spreading of some vital essence of myself* marked an enhancement of her going-on-being, like *a spreading of invisible sentient feelers, as a sea anemone spreads wide its feathery fingers.* A defensive turn inwards did not preserve the self, Milner believed, merely cut it off from the potential to thrive, but I still feared the fragility of those *feathery fingers* spread wide.

One morning at yoga Sally said, *Stay interested in the small movements that go on. Once you are in the pose, observe the shape you are making, and let it be. Breathe into it, don't judge it.* Staying interested in the small things required an attention at odds with my default professional mode – keep on the move, don't take a lunch break, rush from class to meeting to class to meeting, finish one task then start the next straight away – but was much easier here where being aware of how my feet felt on the floor, or how I was holding my shoulders, gave me repeated opportunities to stop, observe, align, breathe. And if I could observe the shape I was making and let it be *here*, could I also do that elsewhere?

23.

Shatterling

I returned to England – once again – in time for the start of the new academic year in late September, the Indian summer compensating somewhat for my departure from New Zealand just as the first signs of spring were emerging there. The juggernaut of the new term picked me up and carried me through the first month back, my feet barely touching the ground it seemed, but I maintained my new resilience and was grateful.

I tried to resume my regular runs and started at a yoga class in a church hall in Sandwich, but the large classes felt soulless after Sally's studio and my attendance petered out. I could feel my shoulders tightening as I spent too many hours at my desk.

On the cusp of winter, the lease on my cottage in Sandwich expired before the new rental flat I had lined up was available, and I had to move into a holiday cottage temporarily. The limbo of the past two years – caught between England and New Zealand, sickness and health, past and future – became unbearably concentrated into that two-week period, surrounded by suitcases and boxes in a twee cottage the size of a studio flat. Now, somehow, there were only two weeks of the teaching term left. In three weeks I was due to fly back to New Zealand for the Christmas break and I was still living out of suitcases. Household detritus like saucepans, coat-hangers and an ironing board were stored in my office on campus.

The temporary cottage was in the hamlet of Shatterling, a name that sounded like something out of a Gerard Manley Hopkins poem and was a suitable adjective for my current state of mind. The morning I was due to move there I was notified by email that I had missed out on a job in New Zealand, after a video-conference interview earlier in the week. Shattering – falling to pieces from a sudden blow – or *scatterling* – a wandering person of dubious character or provenance. Either way, I was well suited for residence in Shatterling.

In the otherwise immaculate bathroom of the cottage there was an unidentifiable stain that repulsed me. You could only see it in a certain light. I couldn't bring myself to clean it off – I didn't want that proximity to it, even through a cloth – but my eyes were drawn to it every time I was in there.

The first two Shatterling nights meant two bottles of wine and two sleeping tablets. I retreated to bed, as I always did when it all became too much, turning in early in the evening, lingering long in the morning. Getting up to make coffee and toast, first at four, then again at nine. Taking it back to bed like returning to a life raft.

Bed is mother, says the Australian writer Helen Garner.

My mother says that I am the only child she has ever known to cry to go to bed. Most children beg to stay up, she says, but when I was small – still small enough to be sleeping in a cot – she would find me standing beside my cot, even during the day, holding on to its rails and crying, saying *I want to go to bed now*. What kind of child does that, I wonder, weeps for the transitional object of comfort, the bed, rather than the first object, the mother?

ᴡ

On the second afternoon in Shatterling, a Sunday, I made the effort to get dressed and sit on the sofa, where I knitted compulsively for five hours watching a re-run of *Cranford*. Those ladies of Cranford knew all about fretwork, too. Outside, it was dark by 5pm.

The previous night I had woken myself from a dream by yelling out in my sleep, something I never did. My daughter, M, had been driving off, laughing, not looking back, in a car packed with friends and all her possessions. I was stricken. I called after her, *You didn't say goodbye before you left!*

I hadn't left the cottage for two days. Exercise – a walk, a run – seemed a distant memory already.

On the third day I decided to go to my office, even though Mondays were usually a valuable day when I could work away from campus and its inevitable interruptions. I needed to be somewhere that seemed familiar, that gave me a routine and a semblance of belonging. In my office, I could prepare for the teaching week, crammed into Tuesdays, Wednesdays, Thursdays, when I knew where I needed to be at certain times, what I needed to do to prepare for those commitments, and could be reasonably confident of fulfilling them without undue mishaps or reversals.

I left the cottage without any makeup – something I never do – as I couldn't face rummaging through suitcases to find my cosmetic bag and feared that, if I delayed leaving, a creeping sense of inertia might make the whole enterprise seem too much trouble and I would go back to bed.

As I drove, the glow of the late-autumn morning sun across the land cast the dips of the bare fields into high relief, and the silhouette of a line of beech trees along a ridge cheered me, as it always did, with the clarity and intricacy of its outlines.

Once in my office I sat at my desk, trying not to kick the laundry basket wedged under there for lack of any other remaining space in the room. I finished writing a lecture, prepared handouts for my seminar classes, replied to copious emails.

Yes, you can come and talk to me on Thursday about your dissertation.

No, I'm sorry but I can't attend your book launch due to another commitment that day but congratulations!

Yes, the marking for that module has been completed.

Yes, I can see you on Wednesday to look over your essay plan.

Yes, I have completed my Time Allocation Schedule. The only problem was that there did not seem to be a category that included the time I needed to allocate to complete the Schedule. Time I could have spent more productively on one of the other categories, like Scholarly Activity.

The soothing banalities of class prep and admin distracted me from my scattered thoughts, my fragmented life, helped by the fact that teaching, not usually the highlight of my working life, had been a pleasant surprise this term. All my classes were attentive and talkative, showing up every week ready to contribute and responding with enthusiasm to the work I set them.

It was not always thus. All the university teachers I know marvel at the strange chemistry of the seminar room: one group is energetic and a pleasure to teach while the next – same course, same material – may be silent and passive, leaving you drained at the end of the session after you have done your utmost to instil some energy and impart something: knowledge, enthusiasm, curiosity, anything to lift the suffocating pall of unknowing that permeates the room.

I find you can usually tell what's in store from the moment you walk into a classroom. If you enter to find a hubbub of chatter, it will be fine. If you walk into deathly silence, your heart sinks.

Last year, for instance, I endured a term where not only was the seminar group sitting in silence when I entered the room, they were sitting in the dark.

Every week.

Every week I entered the room, turned on the lights with mock surprise, and said (I hoped light-heartedly), *Oh, you're sitting in the dark again. Why didn't anyone turn on the lights?*

The ensuing two hours went downhill from there.

Imagine my delight, then, to find that this term I entered classrooms where the students were *already* animatedly discussing the week's topic with each other. In my liveliest class something happened that had never occurred before in more than 20 years of teaching undergraduates. We had worked productively through all the material I had planned for the session and, although it was 10 minutes before the class was due to end, I asked them if they wanted to finish up early today because we had made such good progress. *No,* replied one student, *I'm finding this really interesting. Can we keep going a bit longer?* I feared she might be incurring the silent wrath of her fellow students, that she was the exception in the room, but there were nods and murmurs of assent all around the table. So we continued, even going a little over our usual finish time, before they all packed up their books and laptops and hurried away with their bright-eyed, clear-skinned, youthful energy, still chatting, thanking me as they left. They would never know what they had given me that day.

❦

When I left the office late that Monday afternoon I stopped at the supermarket to buy ingredients for dinner, only to remember that the cooking equipment I would need was currently in a box in my office. The rest of the working week went by in a blur. *This is a low / but it won't hurt you.*

I eased up on the wine and the sleeping tablets and was finally rewarded with a sleep-in at the end of the week. Or a *lie in*, as they say here, which is actually more accurate for me as the best part is not the extra sleep but the luxury of lying in bed – reading, writing, drinking coffee, looking out the window – for as long as I want. But *lie in* is also uncomfortably close to *lying in*. Or *lying in state*. Death or childbirth: not the kind of associations I would like to make with one of my favourite pastimes. It's often the small words, the small things that trip you up, remind you that you are in a strange place.

Small things like a speeding fine, incurred for driving 7 miles per hour in excess of the limit on a road you drive most days and where, on most days, it is impossible to even approach the speed limit because the traffic moves at a crawl. You know that road well, every lamp post, every curve, every sign, the weed flowering in the cracked concrete on the edge of the roundabout, because you have spent extended periods of time contemplating them while you inch forward and calculate how late you will be to the meeting or how long your son will be left waiting in the rain.

But one day, 17 months ago, the road was miraculously clear and I, apparently, reached the fateful speed of 37 mph. I was oblivious to this achievement until, some weeks later, a letter addressed to my husband – already back in New Zealand by then but still the registered owner of the car – arrived at the Sandwich cottage, having been forwarded from our previous village home. The letter contained no details of how to pay the fine, offering instead the opportunity to attend a driver safety course (in the county town over a 90-minute drive away, and on a weekday) and asking for confirmation of the offending driver's identity.

I replied to the letter, informing the county police that I was the driver and that I was replying on behalf of my husband, the registered owner of the vehicle but who was no longer resident in the UK. In due course I received several further letters, repeating the offer of the safety course which, if not taken up by a specified date, would leave no recourse but to pay a modest fine, but still with no information about how this payment might be made. I wanted to pay the fine rather than lose a day's work – and, more significantly, subject myself to the anxiety of a day in an uncertain environment of possible contamination – so I waited for further instructions. Eventually, months later, a letter detailing how to pay the fine arrived. This letter coincided with a dark phase of my breakdown and I neglected it. The fine grew.

Since I had identified myself as the driver, all these letters were now addressed to me at my current address in Sandwich. One day, however, another letter arrived, informing me that I would be required to appear in court to answer a charge of failing to identify the driver of a vehicle involved in a traffic offence. I panicked. After a day of fear-induced paralysis, I managed to phone the number on the letter and eventually spoke to a helpful woman (or so I thought) and explained to her the Kafka-esque absurdity of having received a letter addressed to me personally – contact information that I had provided when I originally acknowledged my culpability as the driver – charging me with failing to provide my identity. The woman checked the file of my 'case' and informed me that, due to the errors in the official correspondence that I had pointed out, my case would be dropped, but I would have to pay the fine, which had now trebled.

I paid it, thankful to have the matter over so I could go back to coping with the ordinary terrors of daily life.

Several months passed, and I received a brief letter from the East Kent Enforcement Centre informing me that a sum of over £800 would be deducted from my next pay cheque to pay a fine. No further information about the offence was provided. Was this some kind of scam? *No*, the woman in the university payroll office I spoke to assured me, they had *been officially notified to deduct the amount* and were *therefore obliged to do so*.

I rang the number on this letter and spoke to an enforcement woman, who could shed little light on the matter other than to say that it seemed to refer to a car-related offence. She told me to call the East Kent court administration for further information. I did.

Press 1 for confiscations, press 2 for victims of crime, press 3 for family, press 4 for payment of fines, press 5 for court administration.

The court administration man told me that the offence, dating back *17 months* and stemming from a speeding fine, was *failing to identify the driver of a vehicle.* Yes, he could see I had paid the fine but this other charge still stood (so the first helpful woman had been wrong?) and my only recourse was to appear before a magistrate to make a statutory declaration affirming that I had received no further correspondence after paying the fine to alert me to the fact that the matter was ongoing. The first available court date was in several weeks' time, but in the meantime, he assured me, the process of compulsory payment would be frozen until the matter was resolved.

Two weeks later my pay slip arrived. Over £800 had been deducted. Payroll confirmed they had received no instruction to forestall the compulsory deduction.

Tim, the courts man (we were on first name terms now), confirmed that, *to be honest, it was very unusual for enforcement to proceed with the compulsory payment when the matter was still outstanding* as it would only create more work for them if the matter was resolved in my favour and they had to refund it.

Despite my best efforts to stay resilient, I was well down the rabbit hole at this point, spinning in a parallel universe of absurdity and contradiction, as if the past three years had never happened and I was still a naïve colonial fresh off the plane who thought that – based on my previous adult life experience up to that point – things like opening a bank account or setting up a new mobile phone number were simple matters. Or that, if you were fined for an offence, you would be fully informed of the details of said offence.

I would never feel at home in this country.

HOW DID THESE PEOPLE EVER RUN A FUCKING EMPIRE? had become something of a catch cry in our household in the early months of our time in England, when either my husband or I had finished yet another bewildering encounter with the bureaucracy of some large institution or other. We frequently needed to vent in this way, to affirm our own shared reality in the face of yet another farcical or illogical practice that had brought us undone, shaken our confidence that as a pair of educated adults we could reassemble our life in a place *where we speak the language, for fuck's sake.*

It often reminded us of our sabbatical in Italy a decade earlier, where we suffered similar issues but had attributed them to the fact that our Italian was rudimentary and everyone knew Italian bureaucracy was unfathomable. Then, we could even regard such problems with a sense of whimsy, especially at the end of the day while we sipped chilled Vernaccia in a warm piazza as the bells chimed and the children ate gelato or chased the pigeons. How amusing that, as a visiting fellow to one of the oldest universities in the world, and the recipient of a generous stipend as part of their visiting fellowships scheme, I could still not be issued with a library card. *Ah, Italy*, we would say.

But England, in my experience, has always been short on whimsy. I would never understand its byzantine ways or the apparent equanimity with which the locals regarded them, their indifference to the fact that in other places – on the other side of the world, for instance – life was immeasurably easier, as if perhaps I was making it up, or there was no point even imagining such simplicity.

Oh, yes, they would say with a shrug, *you have to wait weeks to get broadband installed here.* (Eight weeks; living just over 90 kilometres from London, we had waited eight weeks.)

ᴡ

I gave up contesting my fine. After a final phone call to courts administration I lost any confidence that sanity would prevail and feared that I might not be convincing in challenging the court's paper trail. I felt powerless and cowardly but at least the matter was finally at an end (and I have that in writing). I was still reluctant to test my recovery too much, choosing instead to forgive myself for any culpability in the whole matter (and whatever that may be I will never know now).

An English friend of mine who lived in Rome for some years talks about how living in Italy 'rubbed the rough edges off' him. After a certain period of time there, he says, he realised he could either keep maintaining his own sense of how things should be done and what to expect of daily life – and therefore continue to feel uncomfortable, frustrated, and unhappy – or make his peace as a *straniero* living in a strange place and stop expecting the place to change to fit around him. I wonder whether I will ever come to feel similarly about England; ever feel that instead of being worn down by it I will feel smoothed and shaped, like a pebble in a rushing stream?

I moved to my new flat inside the city walls in Canterbury, in earshot of the cathedral bells. A flat where no one had ever slept in the bed, or cooked in the kitchen. It calmed me to know that. Ten days later, with the final classes of the term over, I was due to fly home to New Zealand for Christmas, a brief taste of antipodean summer and – best of all – my daughter's wedding. And then back to England for the start of the spring term.

How long will my life be divided between two places? Missing one place – and all it represents – while I am in another? Is living always about loss in some form or other? *The art of losing isn't hard to master*, writes Elizabeth Bishop:

> Lose something every day. Accept the fluster
> of lost door keys, the hour badly spent.
> The art of losing isn't hard to master.
>
> Then practice losing farther, losing faster:
> places, and names, and where it was you meant
> to travel. None of these will bring disaster.

The line between *master* and *disaster* is so thin in the emphatic rhyme of Bishop's poem that the poet's insistence on her mastery of loss rings deliberately hollow, a gesture of bravado in the face of life's upheavals. *I miss them, but it wasn't a disaster*, the poet insists, even if we don't quite believe her.

Over the past three years, I had lost houses, cities, a continent, the losses entirely self-inflicted. I had chosen them – having the privilege of choice in such things – unable to foresee the extent of the damage they would inflict. It now felt impossible to know where it was I had meant to travel when I had decided to leave New Zealand, dividing my family in the process as my daughter chose to stay behind, her life now firmly rooted in New Zealand.

In England I had seemed to lose something every day, *losing farther, losing faster*, till there seemed almost nothing left to lose. Some people have a spectacular falling apart. Mine was rather a slow unravelling, like a dropped stitch that passes unnoticed initially, so you carry on following the pattern, everything seemingly intact but – with time and subjected to the right (or the wrong) kind of pressure – a fissure emerges that runs all the way through to the seam, at which point the unspooling accelerates remorselessly. There is a gaping hole in the texture of your relationship with the world. Recovery seems hopeless; the only option seems to be to ditch the whole project.

Now, over time and by a process that was still in many ways opaque, I was no longer depressed and felt part of a world in which I could act and think, and sometimes even touch, without fear. But what about that cold core, that blankness I had so forcibly encountered at the Retreat with Agnes? Was I just masking that again? How would I know if I was still repeating defensive strategies that had been habitual for so long? And could that be why I was ambivalent about returning to New Zealand permanently – because returning to the intimacies of family on a daily basis would threaten that core? I recognised the child described by Winnicott and Green, who tries to live as if there is no mother, no need for dependence on anyone else, because something invaluable had been broken when I was small, leaving me in fear of my own vulnerability. I worry that my newfound resilience is dependent on my isolation, on living alone much of the time, and worry that I have used the physical distance from my family to prevent anything getting too close for comfort.

⚘

The more I tried to figure out what made life worth living, the more questions it raised, the more unknown I became to myself. As well as literary authors, I turned to writers in the psychoanalytic tradition throughout my recovery because of the way they push me to think creatively about health and illness, past and present. The writers who resonate with me are those who reject the reductive, dogmatic version of psychoanalysis and instead reshape or reinvent it for a more contemporary context. My favourite is Adam Phillips (but you knew that by now), who writes:

> What psychoanalysis, at its best, does is cure you of your self-knowledge. And of your wish to know yourself in that coherent, narrative way. You can only recover your appetite, and appetites, if you can allow yourself to be unknown to yourself. Because the point of knowing oneself is to contain one's anxieties about appetite. It's only worth knowing about the things that make one's life worth living, and whether there are in fact things that make it worth living.

As long as we identify or explain ourselves to ourselves by a simple label – I am an OCD-sufferer, a blank depressive – we diminish our prospects for change. Such an identity might explain my present, give a coherence to my narrative, but did not give me anywhere to go or, at worst, only one direction, one outcome to a sad story: death.

At first glance, though, the idea of being cured of your self-knowledge, the importance of *not* knowing yourself seems counter-intuitive. Surely regaining an appetite for life should involve the kind of reconnection, or wholeness, that Virginia Woolf believed was possible through her writing, where insight or knowledge could emerge from pain? And wouldn't such knowledge, at least in part, be a form of *self*-knowledge?

But what if, in seeking to impose a coherent pattern on our identity – the story we tell ourselves about ourselves – we are just perpetuating the stories that brought us to grief in the first place? What would it mean to allow myself to become unknown, not assume I already knew who I was and therefore what I wanted, or needed to do next?

I have come to feel that I need to resist the temptation of the pattern, the simple explanation of my painful present by reference to my past. If, rather than a desire for a seamless or integrated explanation, I choose instead to dwell on the recovery of *appetite* – an unusual word to choose perhaps but one that draws attention to finding through pleasure what interests me and thus what makes life worth living – I will need to accept that whatever I discover in this way will always be transitional, inconclusive. We don't always have the same appetite; we don't always want the same things we had before.

Through trying to put my experience into words, some of the pain *has* been alleviated – in the way that Woolf described. Putting the pain into words gives it a 'wholeness' and, in the process, deprives it of the full extent of its power to hurt me. But it is what is written that is whole, not the person who writes the words – that person remains incomplete, unfolding, evolving. Neither does the wholeness that may come from writing mean that everything has been revealed and fully understood; that writing makes things watertight, impervious to any further hurt. By 'wholeness' I think Woolf means something like integrity, rather than a perfected state of completion, because the process of writing also creates space for other feelings, sometimes little more than a wince of shame or a wisp of desire, just enough to give a sharper intensity to memory or to present experience that had been missing for so long.

And it is because of this that writing also seems to enable some form of acceptance because of the elusiveness of words, the way they seem simultaneously to expose you but never quite capture what you mean, what you feel, what you think. Words draw you on to tease out the threads, follow an inkling or a hunch, or re-describe a feeling or memory in a new way and, in the process, take me far, far away from the searing shame that I associated with writing in my adolescence. Like the narrator of Elizabeth Hardwicke's autobiographical novel *Sleepless Nights*, through writing I felt able to say: *This is what I have decided to do with my life just now. I will do this work of transformed and even distorted memory and lead this life, the one I am leading today.*

24.

Mater

Then my mother died at the Mater.

It was the verge of another spring in southeast England. The snowdrops bloomed in clumps beside the river and the first of the daffodils appeared around the base of the city walls. A grey wagtail returned to the river below my living-room window, in the same spot where I last saw it in December, balanced precariously on a narrow pipe on the waterline, stooping to rinse and ruffle its wings in the river shallows.

I was spending my days in classrooms, as usual, talking of Esther Summerson's childhood trauma, of Dorothea Brooke's passion to live a good life. Or sitting in meetings listening to presentations on outputs and impact and all the other abstractions which the neoliberal university perpetuates. I talked to colleagues – at seminars, at the pub, over coffee – about writing and thinking and feeling. I sat quietly in the stillness of my flat where I could retreat from it all and regain the energy to go out the next day and face it all again.

One mid-March Monday I had woken very early and lay in bed contemplating the day ahead of me: two lectures book-ending the day, one only half-written yet; a meeting; three hours of consultations with students. *Only two more Mondays before the end of term*, I consoled myself.

At 6.30am my phone pinged on the bedside table: *Call me urgently. Mum's in hospital.* When I phoned my sister in Australia, K's voice was low with distress, lacking her usual vivacity. She was out walking the dog, K said, and had just received a call from a doctor at the Mater hospital (which she pronounced, as we do in Australia, *Martyr* hospital) saying our mother had been admitted with severe respiratory problems and the family needed to come urgently. *Only a day or two left*, the hospice doctor had said. As soon as she could get the dog back home, K and her husband planned to set out on the two-hour drive north from Sydney to the hospice.

As I listened to my sister, my Monday evaporated. There would be no lectures. Instead, there would be an early call to my head of department. Then more calls – to K again, to my daughter and my husband, all on the other side of the world from me. I was reeling but a part of me went into automatic mode – I would need to organise teaching replacements, cancel meetings for the rest of the week, book flights and a train ticket. Easier to immerse myself in the practical rather than think about the emotional. All I knew was that I had to get home to Australia.

Two hours passed and I was still in bed, still busy with my phone and laptop.

Finally, I called my father. He was inconsolable, as I knew he would be, as he had been ever since my mother had been diagnosed with MND less than a year ago. We rarely Skyped now without him tearing up, even sobbing, as he tried to talk about her.

Mum, he told me, had been admitted to hospital on Friday. He had told no one over the weekend. He thought it might just be a bad panic attack. *You remember how your mother always has trouble with her breathing when she's anxious, don't you? The doctors are distressing her. She doesn't like being in a big ward, she wants to come home.* When pressed, he was vague on what exactly the doctors had told him, and it did not correspond at all with what my sister had reported of her conversation with the hospice doctor. In the following days he would continue to mull over what he had been told when, still insisting that he did not think it was serious. *What if the doctors are wrong?* he kept saying.

Dad, I said, *the doctors don't summon the immediate family to the hospital for a panic attack. They don't move a patient from a general ward to a hospice for a temporary breathing problem. I'm coming home.*

No, he said, *wait a day or two till we see how she goes.*

Dad, I said, *it will take me a couple of days to get there, even if I leave today. I'm coming. I'll let you know my flight details. M is flying over from New Zealand, too; she will be there tonight.*

Dad wept even more then, as he would throughout the next two weeks whenever he was forced to confront the love, concern, or kindness of others. *I'm sorry*, he would say repeatedly, *I'd be all right if people would stop being so nice to me.*

By lunchtime my plans were in place. I was booked on a flight leaving Tuesday morning, arriving in Sydney on Wednesday night. I decided to keep my student consultation appointments on Monday afternoon, to maintain some normality until my departure. So I went to campus and, for the next three hours, performed in functioning professional mode, listening to the anxieties of students with what I hoped was a sympathetic ear or responding impassively to thinly veiled complaints about the apparently unwarranted low grades I had given them.

I tidied my office desk, returned library books, informed the administrative staff of my absence and then spent the evening packing and cleaning out the fridge and pantry in my flat: I had shopped only two days before so there was much to dispose of. In my addled state, I couldn't think what else to do with all the perishable food other than throw it out, so I carried bags of rubbish down to the dumpster bins, determined to leave a clean flat behind me in the morning.

The next day, walking along the street beside Canterbury West station and wheeling my large suitcase behind me, I saw my train pull away from the platform. The next one would not be for half an hour. I was now in danger of missing my flight.

I queued to collect my booked ticket from the counter, but I had forgotten to bring the reference number with me. *Please*, I implored the ticket attendant, *I'm on my way to catch a flight to my mother's funeral. Isn't there anything you can do?* He was implacable. *No number, no ticket*, he said.

I knew it was hopeless. I knew the system: no reference number, no ticket. I probably didn't even sound convincing. Didn't everyone say they were on their way to their mother's funeral? Just like the string of dead grandmothers that used to plague my first-year students whenever their essays were due, when I first began teaching all those years ago.

And my mother wasn't actually dead yet so it was a lie in any case.

Aware of the restive queue behind me, I moved away from the ticket window and stood helplessly in the station entry for some minutes, knowing I had no choice but to pay again for a new ticket. So I rejoined the ticket queue and then sat on the platform, watching the minutes count down on the platform indicator until the 9.25am finally arrived. Train to St Pancras. Tube to Paddington. Then the Heathrow Express.

Arriving at Heathrow with what I hoped was enough time before check-in closed, I looked in horror at the totally deserted counters. Not a single passenger waiting, not a single staff member behind the row of check-in desks for my airline. I froze. Then I became dimly aware of a man's voice calling from behind me, and I looked around to see a smiling man beckoning to me from the first-class counter, away from the main check-in area. *Hong Kong flight?* he was calling.

Yes! I replied (although, alas, not first-class).

He checked my luggage and presented my boarding passes for the two flights – Heathrow to Hong Kong, Hong Kong to Sydney – as if we had all the time in the world.

Throughout the first flight I was thinking, *Is this a waste of time? Is it too late already?* I turned my phone back on after landing in Hong Kong, but there were no texts from my sister waiting for me. M had messaged to say she had landed in Sydney and was on her way to the hospice. My husband had texted repeatedly from New Zealand, *Are you OK? Any news?*

I kept travelling: I flew the final leg from Hong Kong to Sydney, drove from Sydney to my in-laws on the Central Coast where M was staying, and the two of us continued the next day to the hospital, further up the coast. Still no texts saying it was too late, no apparent change in my mother's condition.

25.

It's
not
like
it is
in the
movies

The burnished sunshine of an autumn morning lit up the landscape as my daughter drove our rental car up the freeway lined by dense bushland. It was almost a year since we had driven this same road to visit my parents. As far as the eye could see, stands of tall eucalypts lined the ridges, dissolving into that familiar blue haze in the distance where it was no longer possible to distinguish distinct trees.

Now I had made it to Australia in time, I wanted that drive to last forever. M is a cautious driver but I hoped she would drive even more slowly; I was dreading what was awaiting me in the hospice, fearing I would not be able to cope, that I would not act in the way expected of me as the eldest daughter of a dying mother.

M already knew what to expect: she had visited twice already in the short time since her arrival from New Zealand and had learnt the routines of the hospice. She had had some time to adjust to the shock of the changed condition of her grandmother and the helpless grief of her grandfather. I felt both grateful and guilty that M was protecting me, careful to prepare me for what I would see. A mother should be the protective one, not the daughter, but it was not the first time my daughter had sustained me in this way.

The day before, M said, Mum had been quite talkative, asking about family members, speaking affectionately to her. M had also told me that, as the afternoon wore on, when she and my father had sat, each side of the bed, holding Mum's hands and fearing each breath would be her last, my mother had suddenly said, *It's not like it is in the movies.*

My daughter had cried at this.

My father, however, misheard her. His hearing was deteriorating and we often had to repeat to him whatever the medical staff said. He would continue to repeat, over and over – to us, to visitors, to the nurses – *She said it's just like it is in the movies.* He desperately wanted to believe that his movie-loving, light-hearted wife was still in there, somewhere. And that what she was experiencing was the sentimental, Hollywood version of death.

My daughter knew otherwise.

But none of us ever corrected him.

The hospice was a single-storey pale brick building surrounded by trees and well-tended gardens, on the very edge of the large hospital campus dominated by several multi-storey blocks and acres of asphalted car parks. I managed to keep my contamination phobia in abeyance by consoling myself with the distance separating the hospice from the main wards where potentially infectious patients might be. The hospice patients were dying, not contagious. Nor did the hospice have that cloying hospital smell that invariably elevates my anxiety levels. As much as it was possible given its purpose, it was an ordinary, homely building.

My mother was in Room 1, the room closest to the nurses' station, for ease of observation: the first room you encountered on entering the hospice, beyond reception, the vending machines and the chapel. It was only later in the week that we realised this was not a random room allocation: Room 1 was reserved for patients adjudged to be ending their stay the soonest.

At first sight, Room 1 seemed full of people: my father, my sister, a nurse and, in the bed, my mother, so altered that I was pleased that the slight commotion with our arrival gave me an unobserved moment to register my shock, swallow my gasp, and then move towards the shrunken figure who lay helpless, struggling for each breath but so sedated that she seemed removed from the rest of the human activity in her room. My daughter, already crying quietly, moved quickly to the bedside to take my mother's hand – a position she had occupied for several hours yesterday afternoon – and I, following M's lead, sat dry-eyed on the other side of the bed and clasped my mother's left hand. I was surprised at the strength of her grasp in response, her withered and vulnerable state belying the pressure and dexterity she was still able to exercise in her hands and fingers. I winced at the sight of her upper arms, covered in purple and claret-coloured bruises left from countless injections over the past few days.

In the room's only armchair, by the window and away from the bed, my father wept, overcome with my arrival and, with it, a renewed sense of the dreadful nature of the circumstances that had brought us all here so suddenly. My sister bustled cheerfully, chatting to the equally cheerful nurse with that light-hearted informality that Australians effortlessly strike up with strangers in conversation, whatever the situation.

Oh, you're the daughter from England! the nurse said to me. Over the coming days, the hospice staff would often refer to *the daughter from England* and *the daughter from Sydney*. They quickly understood who fitted where in the family structure, how far each of us had to travel each day to the hospice, who would be best to approach for information or to pass on updates to the rest of the family.

After the nurse left, quiet descended on the room. Mum's breathing – shallow, erratic, laboured – was mesmerising; my daughter's continued weeping was heartbreaking. I have never felt more useless, unable to know who or how to comfort, what to do, how to feel.

Over the course of the morning, the four of us – K, M, my father and I – would change positions, taking it in turns to hold one of my mother's hands. We would alternate between trivial chat, desultory attempts to make plans for the coming days, and discussions at loggerheads, trying to get straight what the nurse had said and what the doctor had told whom.

My father would one moment be repeating his belief that it had all been a mistake – *medical mistakes happen every day in hospitals*, he said – to openly discussing whether he should start clearing Mum's room out at home. If I was adrift, he was rudderless. Often unable to even approach the bed because of his fear of losing control of his emotions, he would instead share his interior monologue with us from his armchair, retelling stories we had heard a hundred times, extolling Mum's many virtues, asking about the supermarket prices in England, describing the weather, complaining of his tiredness. He asked questions without any real desire for an answer, moving from one topic to another, just a constant flow of talk that left no room for anyone else to think their thoughts, let alone speak.

After what felt like a whole day but had in fact been two hours, the nurses came to change the port that delivered my mother's medication and requested that we all leave the room. Returning to fresh air and sunlight outside the front of the hospice was an unlooked-for relief that none of us dared acknowledge. Instead, we sat side by side on a garden bench, the four of us, drinking vending-machine coffee in merciful silence.

Just across the stretch of car park from where we sat, a large spotted gum tree with sinuous branches of blush-coloured bark took my attention. As long as I kept looking at it, no one was dying. No one was failing to feel the right way about someone dying as long as I kept focusing on the architecture of its branches, the patterns of light and shade on the trunk from the gently moving leaves. About half way up the tree on the main side branch I spotted a galah, its distinctive pink and grey plumage contrasted against the blue sky behind it. It seemed to look back at me.

Then the bird disappeared. Had I looked away? Had I been distracted by something my father said? Had I been thinking about what I could do to stop my daughter's tears?

That galah's gone, I said, almost involuntarily.

Now all of us scanned the tree.

There it is! My daughter pointed to a smaller branch above where I had first seen the bird. But as I looked, I noticed my bird reappear from what must have been a hollow in the branch where I had first seen it, reversing out, tail first, until it perched once more on the branch. There were two galahs, then.

There must be a nest, I said. And then, sure enough, the bird re-entered the hollow, again disappearing from sight, head first.

Ah, galah eggs, my father said. *You wouldn't believe how dull they are. Just boring, plain white eggs. Not what you'd expect from a colourful bird like that.*

I wasn't really listening. Now I had something that I could concentrate fully on – the continuing appearance and disappearance of the bird, followed by its mate, as they took it in turns to enter the nest. In and out, forwards, backwards. Were they incubating eggs? Both male and female galahs share egg-sitting duties. Or were their chicks giving them grief? They reminded me of frazzled new human parents, trying to settle their fractious offspring.

I could have sat there and watched them all afternoon, much preferring to anthropomorphise these wild birds than deal with the human family surrounding me. But soon, our coffees finished, none of us could really delay any longer returning to Room 1.

My mother was dressed in a fresh nightie, her bed straightened, all in order. Except she still struggled for every breath, still seemed only dimly aware of the people and movement around her as M and I resumed our places on either side of the bed, each taking one of her hands to hold. Dad and K chatted for a while. The room fell silent again. Time passed.

For a time, then, my mother seemed more present. Up till this point she had spoken only a few times. She had seemed to register my arrival with M earlier. She had responded in a simple way to the nurses' questions. She asked for water, once or twice.

She told me that she had dreamt of Canterbury the other night. (Was it really only two years ago that my mother had been healthy enough to visit our thatched village house?) I told her that, when I left, the daffodils surrounding the city walls were in the full bloom of early spring. She smiled. Daffodils were her favourite flowers.

I can't remember now whether something was being said among the rest of us, or whether it was just the general sense of sadness in the room that my mother had somehow sensed, but she suddenly announced to us, *I'm not going anywhere yet. You won't get rid of me that easily.*

Her gallows humour, so out of keeping with her frail, semi-conscious state for most of the day, momentarily stunned us all. Then we all managed to laugh in response, my father repeating her words, *You won't get rid of me that easily*, as he shook his head. I could see how much he wanted her words to be true.

Soon after, my father, worn down already by the hospice visits that required him to drive 40 minutes each way to sit and watch his wife dying, went to take a nap in the visitors' lounge, a daily routine the nursing staff encouraged out of concern for his own fragile health.

K and M went in search of some lunch. I was alone with my mother for the first time. I was terrified that she would die while no one else was here. I hadn't had time to become accustomed to her jagged breathing, didn't know that someone could continue in this way for days, possibly weeks. Like my daughter on the previous day, I assumed that it could only be a matter of minutes or hours.

And then suddenly my mother turned her head on the pillow to face me, squeezing my hand, seeming to be fully aware of my presence, and said, *I have always loved you.*

Now I cried.

I don't remember my mother ever saying that to me before, but is that my memory playing tricks on me?

And what did she mean anyway? *I have always loved you* sounded almost defensive, as if there was some doubt about it. Or as if she didn't think *I* believed it?

Why not just *I love you*?

Was *I have always loved you* better or worse than *I love you*?

And why was I thinking about it like this now? What kind of person analyses their dying mother's declaration of love, wondering what the syntax really meant?

She seemed to lose consciousness then, her breathing even more shallow and erratic. I thought the end was near. When my daughter returned, I sent her to wake my father, fearing he would miss Mum's final moments. But Mum kept breathing that afternoon, and we kept sitting with her.

🙢

At around 4pm the doctors arrived for their afternoon rounds. Luke, the senior doctor, sat quietly with Mum at first, touching her arm, observing her closely, talking to her from time to time. There was no sense of rush or urgency in his demeanour, as if time spent with his patients was precious. His two junior doctors stood further away from the bed, reading their notes and following Luke's lead in their quiet attention to Mum. The room felt calmer.

You've just arrived from England, Luke then said, turning to me, and proceeded to give me the full story, beginning with Mum's admission to hospital on the previous weekend. Luke stressed that Mum had made very clear to the medical staff from the outset that she did not want to be put on a respirator and that she wanted to be kept as sedated as possible to quiet her overwhelming anxiety at being unable to draw a deep breath. My mother had been much more lucid in those first few days, able to talk more freely than she could now. *We are here to respect your mother's wishes*, Luke said, *we won't offer any treatment that your mother has refused.*

You must have some questions to ask, he continued.

I must. Like how a lifelong, devout Evangelical Christian had come to express what sounded to me like her right to die? And why my equally devout father had not challenged this? I knew they both opposed euthanasia on principle but we had apparently all entered a twilight zone where the usual rules no longer applied, where Dad wept freely and Mum asserted herself.

Instead, I asked Luke, *How long do you think?*

We can't be sure, he said. *It could be soon, it could be weeks.*

Weeks? I repeated. Surely it couldn't be possible that someone could continue for so long without food (Mum had stopped eating, too), when drawing breath was a constant struggle?

After Luke and the junior doctors left, Dad repeated his theory that this could all be a mistake, maybe Mum wasn't terminal at all.

Could she, could we, really all carry on like this for *weeks*? And in the meantime what should we do right now? It seemed odd that, at the end of the day, we would all just leave the hospice, leaving Mum alone there. As if we had finished our shift and would clock in again tomorrow morning. We talked about what time we would all return in the morning, then Dad drove home and my sister caught the train back to her family in Sydney.

M and I walked back to our car. The pair of galahs was now huddled together, asleep, on the branch above the one containing their nest hollow, as if protecting and comforting each other from the vagaries of family life. My daughter drove us to the B&B where we planned to stay for the rest of the week, the same one where we had stayed a year ago with K. That evening we drank too much wine and beer, cried, talked, cried some more, and then shared a bed because we didn't want to be alone that night. I woke at six to the sound of raucous kookaburras just outside the window. I smiled, before I remembered where I was and why I was here.

26.

Room 1,
Day 2

Next morning M parked the car in the same place on the same side street as the day before and we walked again across the hospital car park to the hospice, where I looked up to see the two galahs in the spotted gum, one on nest duty – popping in and out of the tree hollow – the other on an adjacent branch, looking down on us.

At reception M and I turned right, along the short corridor to Mum's room. Only day two of my stay and it already felt like a well-established routine. M and I each hugged Dad, back in his customary place in the armchair, then we took Mum's hands, kissed her forehead, and sat in the straight-backed chairs, one on either side of the bed.

Mum seemed groggier this morning, barely able to articulate a greeting to us or any acknowledgement that she knew we were there. The squeeze of her hand was not so firm today.

Over the course of the morning, however, she would come to the surface of consciousness every now and then, with a sense of urgency about something she wanted to say.

Did that woman get her eggs the other night?

What, Mum? What do you mean? I said.

Did she get her eggs the other night? she repeated, more insistently, expending more effort.

Mum, it's all right, there are no eggs. I tried to reassure her. *It's fine, don't worry about it.*

What's she talking about? my father said. His deafness, compounded by his distance from the bed, meant I had to repeat it to him several times before he understood.

Eggs? he said. *What's she talking about?*

I don't know, I replied. *She seems to be wandering a bit. Maybe it's the increased medication.*

Eggs? he continued, reluctant to let the matter drop, as if this was an enigma that it was important to resolve. *When we lived in our first house we used to keep hens and I would sell eggs to the neighbours,* he said. *Maybe that's what she's talking about.*

That was over 50 years ago.

They were on his head, Mum said.

What? said my father. *On his head? What's she talking about?*

My daughter and I exchanged looks across the bed. Where to begin? Which ailing parent/grandparent to deal with first?

It's all right, Dad. She's confused. It's probably the drugs.

But he kept musing, under his breath – although his hearing problem meant he spoke loud enough that he was still clearly audible – *Eggs on his head? Why is she worrying about that?*

It was going to be a long day.

After a quiet interval, during which Mum seemed to be dozing, she turned her head towards me and said, *Will the banner fit in the boat?*

As with all these cryptic comments, it took several repetitions, questions, clarifications, where I would repeat back to her the key words or phrases, in case I had misunderstood – her voice had changed into a higher, thinner, more childlike register – before I could be sure that what I had heard, however absurd, was in fact what she had said.

During these repetitions Dad would be trying to pick up the conversation, looking to me for an explanation that I could not provide.

Boat? What boat? he said. *Your mother doesn't like boats, never has. She went on a boat out to the Sydney Heads once*, he said.

I knew she had been on many boats, despite her fear of water, even a channel ferry and a cruise down the Rhine, so why my father hit upon this particular boat trip, again more than 50 years ago, I had no idea.

M and I wanted to soothe my mother, make her feel that we were listening, but my father clung to the hope that there was a clear truth she was trying to communicate, that because of their long-intertwined lives, perhaps, the key to her true meaning lay in the distant past.

Later in the morning K arrived. She and my father had gone to make cups of tea, and M to seek some fresh air. I was momentarily alone with my mother again.

All the shops are different, she said, *so they're all different lengths.*
Are they? I said.
Yes, she said, before dozing off again. Minutes passed.
That man out there was being awful to that woman, she said then.
What man, Mum?
That man. He was awful.

Eggs and boats and shops seemed harmless enough but it was piteous to see her thoughts wandering toward more distressing subjects – memories? – that were real only to her, far from the hospice room and the beautiful blue sky and lush green ferns just outside her window.

A baby? she said then, a sadness in her voice now, different to the anxious tone that her distressed breathing often caused.
What baby, Mum? There's no baby here.

Was it best to deny the reality of this baby? Or to try to discover its source? Did she even know?

❧

Nurses came and went, a family friend visited and embraced Mum, weeping, before taking my place by the bed to hold Mum's hand. I heard my mother tell her friend that she loved her and I heard her friend softly reciting Bible verses to her. Then Dad and the friend left the room to pray together.

The morning passed. Dad went to the visitors' lounge for a nap. K, M and I continued to sit around the bed, not talking much. Mum became more restless and the nurse came in to settle her, telling us it might be best if we left her for a while, that patients sometimes could sleep more deeply if they were left alone.

Down past the nurses' station, along the second corridor, we walked to the visitors' lounge to find Dad now awake, sitting in the darkened lounge.

I opened the curtains, letting in the light and the breeze through the full-length windows that were found in every room in the hospice, opening out onto a courtyard garden. The four of us sat in the oversized fake leather armchairs, unsure what to do next, taking it in turns to check on Room 1 and report back the reassuring news that Mum now looked peaceful and comfortable, sleeping deeply.

Once again we talked over our plans for tomorrow, taking for granted that the current arrangements would continue: Mum would hang on, Dad would drive down from their home, M & I would stay at the B&B, K would continue to travel up each day from Sydney.

I'm going to get here earlier tomorrow, Dad announced.

We all nodded.

So I can get a good parking space, he added.

A shocked pause – did he just say that? – then we all laughed. Dad looked puzzled. What had he said? Like many men of a certain age, the quest for the good parking space was always a priority, even when your wife was dying in a hospice. Throughout the surreal days we spent gathered at the hospice, there were so many conversations like this. Dad would one moment be fondly describing Mum's sense of style, then the next asking if he should start throwing out her clothes. *Should I call the funeral director?* he asked, more than once. *She's not dead yet, Dad!* one of us would say, exasperated. He had no more idea what to do than the rest of us.

There was no still point, no respite from the pull of conflicting emotions and loyalties as I watched my mother die, my father grieve, my daughter weep and my sister and I keep up appearances, keep functioning as if life was predictable and able to be scheduled. All the time I was thinking, *What am I feeling? What should I be feeling?*

When we all returned to Room 1, Mum was awake again and agitated. The more she struggled for breath, the more distressed she seemed to become; the greater her distress, the harder it was for her to breathe. The nurses were in and out, checking on her, trying to calm and reassure her. We asked if she could be given more medication. The nurse went to check with the doctor.

Help me, I can't breathe, Mum said, in her reedy child's voice. Over and over.

She didn't want her hands held any more; she was fidgeting, restless, pulling at the oxygen tube in her nostrils, still finding enough strength in her fingers to pluck at the bedcovers.

After what felt like an age but must have been half an hour, the next dose of sedation was administered and, 20 minutes later, she was calmer again.

I'm going to have a long sleep then I will see Jesus and that will be all, Mum said.

27.

My heart
in
hiding

Overnight M decided that she needed to return home to New Zealand. She was worn out with grief and anxiety, in a fragile state that worried me, so I booked her a flight home and, next morning, drove her to the nearest station to catch a train to Sydney airport.

When I arrived at the hospice, I was surprised to find that Mum had been moved from Room 1. She was now in a room on the corridor furthest from the nurses' station and next to the visitors' lounge where we had sat with my father the previous afternoon.

When Luke came to see Mum that day, he reiterated that she could continue like this for longer than anticipated. *Your mother's condition hasn't deteriorated since she was moved to the hospice last Monday,* he said, *so we could be talking about weeks.* I inferred from this that the move to Room 19 was also an indication that the assessment of Mum's condition was not quite as grim now.

Despite Luke's reassurance, though, it was clear that Mum's sedation had been increased. She was barely conscious at all and so for much of the day we sat outside her room in the warm autumn sunshine, keeping an eye on the bed through the French windows. As it was the weekend, my sister's husband was here too, and the three of us chatted quietly, appreciating the respite from the distress of the previous afternoon while we tried to absorb the possibility of a much longer duration than anyone had anticipated. My father, now struggling with a chest infection, only came to the hospital briefly in the afternoon, unable to stay away for the whole day as we had recommended, urging him to spend a day in bed resting.

Just once that day, while two nurses were checking my mother, adjusting her position in the bed and ensuring that the medication port was still in place, she rallied slightly. *Unassuming*, she said.

Unassuming? one of the nurses repeated.

Unassuming, said Mum again, nodding slightly.

🜊

The next day was much the same: K, her husband and I sitting in the courtyard. Currawongs warbling in the large shade tree above us, the last warmth of summer still lingering.

My father preferred to sit inside, in the armchair as usual. He had arrived before the rest of us and had found Mum again in a distressed state. In despair, he had sung her the first verse of her favourite hymn (my father is not a singer and was still struggling with a chesty cough). Unbelievably, he reported that she had responded by singing the chorus. Mum had always had a strong soprano voice, a source of embarrassment to me in my adolescence when I sat beside her in church every week.

It was especially hard to believe my father's account of this hymn singing as my mother was now deeply sedated, saying little, only occasionally asking for a sip of water, or saying *Pillows out, pillows out!* when she wanted a pillow removed, or *Up!* when she wanted the incline of the bed adjusted, or *On my side, on my side!* when she wanted to turn over. These demands had a needy insistence, stripped of any adult dignity, like a small child pleading for help *now, right now*.

My father was exhausted and clearly unwell so he only stayed a couple of hours before driving home, knowing that his two daughters would remain, and that the immediate crisis seemed to have passed.

My sister, too, was worn down by the strain of the past week and the daily travel – she had three children at home and had just returned to her studies a month previously – so I encouraged her to take a day off from visiting tomorrow, knowing that my father and I would be here. I would call her if anything changed.

ᴡ

Exactly a week after I had received that early morning text from my sister, the two galahs were again perched on their nest branch when I arrived at the hospice. Another day of blue sky and warmth.

Again, I found my father in the armchair and Mum in a state of deep sedation. I pulled a chair up close to Dad – so he could hear me better – as it seemed unlikely that Mum would be aware of anyone sitting close beside the bed today.

The morning passed slowly. Nurses came and went. Dad made a cup of tea. I had not been able to eat anything during the days at the hospice. I had no appetite and just drank water till I left in the late afternoons.

A hospital volunteer, a grey-haired woman, came in and offered to bring some flowers to Mum's room. I waved her aside, not wanting to talk to anyone, but she was insistent. *I come in every Monday*, she said, *and bring flowers from my own garden, just to cheer up the rooms a little.*

OK, thank you, I said, feeling it would be easier to acquiesce, and the volunteer looked pleased. She quickly returned with a spray of yellow rosebuds in a small vase that she placed on the shelf above Mum's bed, before leaving Dad and me alone again.

In the early afternoon, Mum became agitated again. *Up!* and *Pillows out!* and *On my side, on my side!* Over and over. She would try to turn herself, grabbing onto the bedrails with weak but determined hands. The nurses had told us not to move her ourselves, that she would only want to be moved back again in a few minutes, and that we needed to be careful with her tubes and catheter. But in the face of her distress and her now almost constant demands to be moved, somehow, anyhow, I tried to help her, although nothing seemed to give her comfort. Now she began to dig her hands down into the bed, beside her thighs, trying to force herself to sit up. My father and I were surprised by her determination and the apparent strength she could muster to do this.

Her diaphragm muscles were giving out but somehow she could still support her body weight – at least momentarily – with her arms.

Her agitation continued for much of the afternoon. She would seem to settle for a while but after 20 minutes or so she would be keen to move again. *On my side, on my side!* It was like dealing with a headstrong toddler, and I was struck by a kind of absurdity in our futile efforts to accommodate her, her emphatic insistence on being able to shift her position. She wasn't complaining about breathlessness, she wasn't feebly saying *Help me, help me*, the way that she had previously, as if we were cruelly refusing to come to her aid. There was a kind of desperate strength in her actions that afternoon that distracted my father and me from what they might signal.

By mid-afternoon, after a further dose of sedation, Mum finally seemed to settle more, dozing briefly, so my father left. I knew he would drive home and be in bed by 7pm.

My mother and I were alone. She was quieter now but I was still unnerved by her agitation and didn't want to leave her. If she stirred again, how long might she struggle in the bed, trying to turn herself, or calling *Up! Up!* to no one?

Like my father, I'm no singer but, at a loss, I began to hum 'In My Life', of all things. I have no idea why. It is not a song I had thought about for years but Mum had introduced me to the Beatles from earliest infancy. And I may have imagined it but Mum's breathing seemed to become a little calmer, a little deeper. So I hummed it again. And again.

⚘

It was almost peaceful in the room now. No activity in the corridor outside the room. I sat beside the bed, trying not to think ahead, trying not to think at all.

Mum roused herself at one point and tried to take off her wedding ring to give to me.

No, Mum, I said, *you keep it.*

But she was insistent, slipping the ring easily off her finger, so much thinner now after all the weight she had lost in recent months. I put the ring in my handbag for safekeeping, not wanting to challenge her, planning to give it to my father tomorrow.

She settled again.

A bit later, she said, *Look after your Dad.*

I will, don't worry, I said.

More time passed. I was inert, reluctant to move, as if it might break the spell of the calm now present in the room.

With her eyes still closed then, Mum said, *No more pain. No more death. No more death.*

She was quiet again.

No more death. No more death. No more death, she repeated.

I could think of nothing else to say except to repeat her words back to her. *No more death*, I said.

And then I said, *It's OK to go now, Mum, if you want. It's OK. No more death.*

I had not planned to say that. I had a dim idea that people said that sort of thing but was it for me or for her that I said it?

When I left around five, more reassured now that she was resting peacefully, I told her I would see her tomorrow.

My sister called me at 5.30am. The hospice, unable to reach Dad, had called K to say that Mum had deteriorated and was in distress. We needed to come now. K was more than two hours away in Sydney. *I'm on my way*, I said.

In the time it took me to dress, K called again. The hospice had called her back to say it was too late.

My sister's voice was hollow.

Dad was not answering his phone, for some reason, so he had not yet been notified. I decided to drive to the hospice anyway, in case Dad might be on his way, unaware of what awaited him.

After phone calls to my daughter and my husband, it was almost 8am by the time I arrived at the hospice. Luke was writing notes at the nurses' station and he greeted me kindly, coming around the desk to place a hand on my shoulder and offer his sympathies. I asked if Dad had been contacted yet.

Doesn't he know? Luke asked.

No, the duty nurse replied. *We have been calling but his phone is not answering.*

I'll try again now, Luke said.

I stood, then, and listened as the doctor gave the news to my father that his wife had died, a conversation no child ever wants to overhear. As I listened, though, I noticed a discrepancy in the narrative Luke relayed to Dad. Looking over Mum's chart as he spoke, Luke said that the night nurse had checked on Mum and found her dead in her bed at 5am.

So what was the truth about the hospice call to K at 5.30am saying, *she's deteriorating, please come*, followed by the next call at 6am? Was Luke mistaken, somehow misreading Mum's notes, or was this some kind of protocol at the hospice, to summon the family in a way that avoided giving the news of the loved one's death as a fait accompli, as if to soften the blow, and prepare us for the fateful call soon to follow?

I thought back to Mum's agitated state yesterday afternoon and dreaded to imagine that she might have suffered alone like this, in the early hours of the morning, no one to hear her distress, to be there by her side as she struggled to breathe, to be able to reassure her, *No more pain. No more death*. It was an unbearable thought that would continue to plague me. I never told anyone else in the family my fears about the conflicting narrative of events reported by the nurse and the doctor.

Luke then said to my father, *Your daughter is here now. Would you like to speak to her?* and passed the phone to me. Normally, I don't like to use public phones, phones used by other people, people who tend the sick and dying. This was not a normal time.

Dad was weeping uncontrollably, not able to say much.

I'll be there as soon as I can, Dad, OK? I said. *I'll just finish up here and then I'll be on my way, OK?*

Luke then took me aside and asked if I would like to see my mother. She was still in her room, he said. I could go and see her. *Take as much time as you want*, he said.

I knew that neither my sister nor my father wanted to view the body – it was something they had already made clear – so I felt that at least one of us should see her.

Even though I knew the way by now, Luke escorted me around the corridor to Room 19, opening the door for me and repeating, *Stay as long as you want.*

The door closed behind me and I was in a darkened room – no overhead lights on today, the curtains drawn across the glass doors, blocking out the morning sun that bathed the courtyard. The fan that had been running constantly over the past few days (to create a feeling of plentiful airflow that helped some patients feel less anxious about their breathing difficulties, the nurses had said) was quiet now.

I put my bag down on the nearest chair and then pulled back the bed curtains.

There she lay. Perfectly still. No more oxygen tube in her nose. The bed no longer elevated and no more muddle of pillows. Just one smooth pillow beneath her head and the bedcovers neat and tightly tucked in. She was dressed in a fresh nightie, her hair combed, the skin on her face smooth and shining, as if freshly moisturised. Her hands were lightly clasped across her lower abdomen, one of the yellow rosebuds from the volunteer's vase now placed between her fingers.

And it was my mother, cold and dead.

How often had I read that line in *Bleak House*, my eyes pricking, when the abandoned daughter, now an adult, is finally reunited with her mother, too late. It catches me every time, that moment of recognition that is also the realisation of their separation forever.

For a moment I was transfixed by the incomprehensible sight before me. I had never seen death before. And then I burst into involuntary tears, pacing restlessly around the room. I couldn't stand still. There was no one to see me, so I kept crying, walking from one side of the bed to the other, one end of the room to the other.

After – how long? – some minutes, I realised I hadn't yet touched her. Standing close to the bed now, I touched her chest and throat, exposed above the neckline of her nightdress. Cold. And then her hands, the fingertips already yellowing, like the flower she held. Despite this, she still looked lifelike, not least because her mouth was wide open, as if taking in air. Of course this was an unmistakable sign of death, but I kept imagining I could hear a soft intake of breath through her open mouth.

I talked to her some, then, and in talking I felt the irrefutability of her death. Nothing I could say now would create a response, my words went nowhere, meant nothing. I can't recall now what I said. I only remember saying *Oh Mum.*

I was alone in that room and no one else would share what I had seen. No one else in my family would have that memory that, in the first week, came to me every time I closed my eyes: my mother's face in death, smooth, cold and immobile, wide open mouth, closed eyes.

I don't know how long I stayed in that dim room. I might have stayed longer if I had not been worrying about Dad, feeling the need to drive to him as soon as possible.

I left Room 19 for the last time, noticing as I closed the door again that a sign on the door said *No visitors. Please go to nurses' station.* I walked past Luke and his junior doctors without a word, and as I turned the corner to the exit I noticed that Room 1 was also in darkness, door closed, also displaying the sign *No visitors. Please go to nurses' station*, so I knew the fate of the patient who had replaced Mum there just a few days ago.

I made myself look for the galahs in the spotted gum, knowing this was the last time I would cross this carpark, and was grateful to see them again, side by side, huddled together asleep.

28.

Stirred
for a
bird

The next day I woke at 5.15 after a full eight hours of uninterrupted sleep. When had I last done that? Swimming up towards full consciousness, I tried to remember where I was. Not my flat in England, not the B&B on the inlet, but now at my in-laws, where M, my husband and our son were due to arrive from New Zealand tomorrow. For the next week, I would work through this list of places again each morning when I woke, feeling the disorientation afresh each time, just as each night, as I tried to fall asleep, I would see my mother's face as it was after death in the darkened hospice room.

The plovers are already awake and on patrol in the pre-dawn darkness. I can hear them pass overhead with their raucous *kee-kee-kee* call. I have seen them everywhere this week: beside the motorway, in the field next to my parents' house, on the grass by the water's edge at the B&B, and here at my in-laws'. The plover or masked lapwing – a name that sounds like a superhero from a sub-Marvel franchise – usually lays its eggs after rain, and the east coast of Australia had had record rains shortly before my arrival. Plovers nest on the ground in open areas so they can see their predators and take defensive action if they detect intruders – swooping and diving, calling aggressively, anything to deflect the intruder from the vulnerable eggs. *If you cannot avoid the area,* one bird book advises, *try not to walk directly towards the birds or make eye contact with them.*

After the plovers, the little wattlebirds soon join in the dawn chorus, along with the constant background chatter of the rainbow lorikeets, circling in flocks or scattered through the stand of she-oaks by the lake where my in-laws live. Then the sulphur-crested cockatoos wheel by, screeching and screaming, sounding *as if they're ripping books to shreds.*

I read in bed for a while, the first time I have opened a book since sitting on the plane before take-off at Heathrow. After breakfast I walk the footpath that winds beside the lake. No need any longer for the morning hospice routine.

The fine weather has broken; it has rained heavily overnight and the rain will continue in intermittent deluges over the remainder of the week. But this morning the bush has that washed-clean feel, the smell of wet earth and eucalyptus leaves mingling with the salty tang of the lake shore. All week I have been driving past bushland on the way to and from the hospice, at high speed on the motorway. Now I can see things up close, stopping to watch a flock of black swans feeding on a weed bed in the shallows of the lake, or to contemplate a kookaburra on a low branch, eying me warily as I distract him from his pursuit of insects and lizards in the undergrowth.

As the path winds through a thicker stand of trees, ancient gums rising up a hillside beside the lake, the air is suddenly full of the sound of bellbirds *sweeter than singing … running and ringing.* I have never heard so many, such a constant calling. When we first read Henry Kendall's most famous poem in primary school, I had never heard one at all, despite living in such a bird-rich environment in coastal New South Wales. The bellbirds I hear now – bell miners, actually, and not to be confused with korimako – are the descendants of Kendall's nineteenth-century birds: his cottage remains, less than a mile from where I am standing.

In Wordsworthian vein, Kendall's poem marks a memory of
bellbirds – *Often I sit, looking back to a childhood / Mixt with the sights
and the sounds of the wildwood* – and ends with a wish that, although
far from the idyllic landscape of his youth, he might be able to write
poetry with the power to charm, *to slumber the pain of my losses / With
glimpses of creeks and a vision of mosses.* With its insistent rhythms, neat
rhymes and romanticised vision of the Australian landscape, Kendall's
poem did indeed charm me as a child. I'd never read Wordsworth
then, but my own literary landscape was thoroughly anglicised so
Kendall's *sycamore bowers* and *sunbeams* sounded just right to me, and I
didn't notice that the poem had to explain to its readers that October
in Australia was the equivalent of *May-time*.

All this week I have been encountering birds protecting their
defenceless young, seeing the lengths they will go to in order to
preserve the precarious life of eggs and nestlings. The musical call of
Australian bellbirds is also a protective strategy, defending their habitat
and their food source from other birds. The constant *ping* sound,
a single metallic-like note made by each bird in a colony, makes a
tinkling sound en masse, continuing throughout the day and carrying
far through the bush. It is a magical sound to immerse yourself in but
you almost never see the bellbirds themselves.

On this walk I am happy – alone, in the company of birds,
between the lake shoreline and the thick green bushland. The *pain
of my losses* charmed asleep? Or not yet awoken or acknowledged? I
feel guilty that I am happy; yesterday, I wept over my mother's dead
body, visited my distraught father, then drove for 90 minutes through
such torrential rain that I could barely see the road in front of me, my
shoulders tensed with anxiety as other vehicles nonchalantly sped by
me. And I know that the next few days will be gruelling: more visits
to my father, tense negotiations about the format of the funeral, calls
to family friends to notify them, then the funeral on Saturday. But
right now, right here, I am happy.

A pair of whipbirds call – the male's long, ringing high note
followed by a 'whip crack' sound, then the female's string of more
melodic *choo-choo-choo* notes. In my childhood – when I heard this call
every day from the bush around our house – I used to think it was
made by a single bird, not realising it was a duet.

I greet other walkers I pass, mostly residents of the many retirement villages scattered around the lake, like my in-laws. A pair of grey-haired women walking their elderly Welsh terrier laugh at me: *We saw you take that photo of the kookaburra, darl.* What a cliché: a kookaburra, such an everyday, unremarkable bird to anyone but a tourist. Hardly worth a photograph. And my iPhone had only given me a grainy image, lacking sufficient zoom to capture the sky-blue feathers patterned across the grey-brown wings of the bird or its large beady eye. Just a sharp-beaked shape perched on the grey-green needle-like foliage of a she-oak branch, against a background of silver-blue water.

29.

Someone's badness

To my shame, I do not cry at my mother's funeral. I am afraid of succumbing to another relapse and slipping back into depression and hopelessness; tears could be the start of such a process. But later that day, battling the remnants of a cold I had picked up in my travels, there is so much congestion in my head that I have to pull it from my nostrils in thick yellow strands until I feel depleted and disgusted.

The day after the funeral I fly back to New Zealand with my family. I wait for grief to manifest, as everyone assures me it will. It is like waiting for an infection to develop, a tired and headachy feeling that leaves me reluctant to throw myself into normal activities. I approach each day gingerly. But I walk the dog, and I return to yoga, at first stiff and inflexible, then gradually less fragile, more receptive.

The kingfishers return to the ridge and valley in the early autumn, just as they did last year. The goats begin to grow their winter coats; almost overnight Marjoram has transformed into a silky, bleached blonde. Myrtle, the little one (and my favourite), has grown quite portly since I last saw her. She is evidently winning the battle of the food buckets. Pansy is still the most eager to be patted, or rubbed behind her ears in the way that cats like, too.

I am home in Matakana for a few weeks only, on compassionate leave. I will soon be uprooted, dislocated, again.

The poet Diana Bridge writes:

> If you want more than to brush your face
> against nature, eyes clinging briefly to swatches
> of sky …
>
>   if you want more
> than the quick epiphany of a hill line
> breaking free of houses, you have to
> walk the same route each day.
>
> ….
>
>   to read the sharp calligraphy
> of birds carved on the air, to ambush
> nature into telling, you need to stay
> in one place for more than a year.

I can't seem to do that, stay in one place for more than a year. Part of me wants to, another part wants what lies on the other side. Some days it feels like half a life, other days like two good lives, rich with choice and opportunity. Sometimes I revel in it, sometimes I feel guilty – about the distance from family, the air miles I clock up, the endless procrastination about life versus career.

Have I learned by now to tolerate some of my own badness, in order to take some fear out of the world? Maybe. Fear is not such a dominant presence in my life now. And I know I have recorded here many instances of badness, failures of feeling or behaviour, so I guess that means I am tolerating it more. When I first wrote down that quotation about *some of one's badness*, I transcribed it wrongly. I had written 'someone's badness' – someone else's badness, in other words, not mine. Mine was so intolerable then, apparently, that I could not even write it down.

I watched someone else's badness in Westgate Gardens in Canterbury, a few days before I was so suddenly called home to Australia. Walking behind a woman, I saw her stoop to pick the budding daffodils newly dotted across the grass beneath the riverside trees. And then, even more brazenly, she also took a fresh bunch of mixed flowers that had been left on the plinth of a memorial. She kept walking through the gardens with her bouquet of stolen blooms, displaying her badness for all to see. I was shocked and angry. But I was also cowardly. I said nothing. I did not confront her. I walked silently behind her, as if I saw nothing. So there was some of my badness evident in the park that day too.

When I was small my mother would volunteer me to present bouquets to eminent visitors at the parish church we attended in suburban Sydney. And then one day I refused to present any more flowers. I had become terrified of the public display – walking up to the front of the church or the stage of the church hall, weighed down by the heavy bouquet, the eyes of the congregation on me. So one day I said no more; I didn't want to do it; *please don't make me do it*. My mother was angry; she had loved dressing me up for these occasions. I was sad to disappoint her. I didn't mean to be naughty, I was just scared.

A parent is someone who has the power to expose a child to danger: a painful but unavoidable consequence of the parent–child relationship when every child is born defenceless, vulnerable, powerless. How parents understand that power and choose to respond to it (assuming they do choose, that they are not simply re-enacting patterns from their own dangerous childhoods) is what determines so much of our experience as humans. In refusing to be the flower-bearer any more I had identified as a danger something that my mother considered a favour, a pleasure for us both. I couldn't understand why she would want me to do something that made me feel scared and exposed.

Such a small incident, its resonance seemingly out of proportion with the bare facts of a simple misunderstanding between mother and daughter. The everydayness of the contact between a mother and child doesn't need to result in sensational acts of mistreatment to leave us diminished, to leave a lingering effect on who we are, how we see ourselves in the world. Somehow – through such small incidents? – I learned two lessons that have stayed with me, to my cost. I learned to fear the world; and I learned to conceal my fear, along with other feelings, and try my best not to need anything or anyone. To look after myself. Because if other people didn't understand that you needed protecting – that you weren't just being naughty but felt your small self was in some kind of danger – then you couldn't really rely on them to look after you.

It could seem like a cruel irony that, through my childish attempts to look after myself, to be self-sufficient, I developed symptoms of phobia, so wary of danger and desperate to protect myself that I feared situations that held no real danger. And the self-recriminations following such frequent episodes of groundless fear led in turn to hopelessness and depression which, in turn, left me vulnerable to OCD.

These responses, these symptoms, I now think, were a signal that I had compartmentalised things – feelings, memories, needs, desires – that I needed to acknowledge as part of myself, that I couldn't keep pushing away, blanking out. Some part of me *was* trying to take care of me, just not in the way that I had developed through my childish strategies of blankness and avoidance. *Pay attention*, part of me was saying, *feel something*. Excessive (obsessive) self-protection was a form of self-care, just not a very good one. Instead, a different kind of awareness was needed, the kind that Sylvia Plath described in her poem 'Tulips'. *And I am aware of my heart*, Plath wrote, *it opens and closes / Its bowl of red blooms out of sheer love of me*.

It wasn't enough to escape to books, or to look to nature for consolation or comfort, although it is clear to me now that both these strategies, too, I learned from my parents: books from my mother; nature from my father. If I couldn't feel at home in my body – without fearing it was going to betray me by its manifestations of panic or fear – then how could I ever really feel at home anywhere else, no matter how far I travelled or how many times I moved house?

On my last visit to my parents' house before I left Australia after my mother's death, I looked through all the family photo albums again. It filled in time in those first days of Dad's bereavement and allowed the two of us to concentrate on something other than his overflowing grief for a while. He liked me to be there with him but he was self-conscious about his emotions, so we both liked the distraction of memories in these manageable forms: yellowing polaroids, curling black-and-white snaps, school photographs, studio portraits.

Here were the professional portraits that Mum had commissioned from a local photographer, taken first when I was a baby and then again as a toddler, re-touched to make my cheeks rosy and my eyes periwinkle blue. They had been prominently displayed in frames around our house when I was growing up. Here were the photographs of me alone in the garden – playing on my swing, or dressed up for Sunday School prize-givings. Here were the photographs of my father awkwardly holding me as a new baby (that my mother had taken with her own Box Brownie camera). But what about my mother and me together?

I was looking for photographs of my mother holding me as a baby. I found only two. One black-and-white photograph shows my mother and grandmother standing side by side, each dressed in austere early-1960s tweed suits in Gran's front garden. My mother is holding me. Both women look stiff and awkward; their almost matching suits at odds with the sense of distance between them that the photograph suggests. I am merely a frilly white thing with a chubby, bonneted face, my limbs obscured under all the ruffles and flounces. I was a winter baby and it looks like a chilly day so I must have been very young when this picture was taken.

The other photograph is in colour. I am on my mother's knee. All of her that can be seen is her left hand holding me upright, her wedding ring clearly visible, and the pattern of her dress covering her lap. I'm pretty sure I remember that that was a maternity dress. So this photograph may record the first of the many failed pregnancies that occurred between my birth and that of my younger sister, seven years later. I am between six and nine months old, I would judge, wearing a white dress with short puffed sleeves and delicate light-blue embroidery across the yoke. My chubby, pink, bare foot pokes out from the frilled hem of my dress. It was evidently a warm summer's day, and the blurred outline of tree trunks can be glimpsed in the background. A picnic, probably. I am looking towards my mother – rapt, engaged. My mouth is open in that way I remember from my own children, as babies, at that cooing, gurgling stage, pre-speech. She holds my whole attention. I am enchanted. I am loved.

Afterword

For the present when backed by the past is a
thousand times deeper than the present when it
presses so close that you can feel nothing else.

VIRGINIA WOOLF

In the grip of phobia, the present does indeed press so close that
you can feel nothing else; all else is blacked out, blanked out. You are
confined to the moment, but not in any Zen-like way, far from it. It is
a kind of freeze-frame, a freeze that burns, that hurts, that scars.

Phobias are 100 per cent reliable: they give you that same
inescapable, insufferable episode of fear and pain again and again. And
the insidious message that is left after that moment has passed – and
it always does pass even though you never believe it will – is: *this will
happen again. Watch out. Be careful. Ever vigilant.*

In my darkest depression in England, I had wanted nothing more
than to return to New Zealand and be left alone to live simply on
the ridge above the ocean. Despite this, I had spent the last three
years flying back and forth, going through the relapses and reversals
of recovery alongside the questioning and uncertainty about career
versus creativity, about what the purpose of my life was and what it
could be.

Now I am well again and medication-free. A year has passed since my mother's death. And I am going home, for good – in every sense, I hope.

Towards the end of her life and suffering from terminal cancer, the queer theorist Eve Sedgwick wrote movingly about hope. *Often a fracturing, even a traumatic thing to experience,* she wrote, hope can energise us *to organize the fragments* that we encounter or create. Because we have the capacity *to realize that the future may be different from the present, it is also possible* – if painful – for us to consider *that the past, in turn, could have happened differently from the way it actually did.*

But – wait a minute – how could hope be 'traumatic'? Because, Sedgwick says, it takes away the certainties of despair, it presents us with the prospect of life, it dares us to take the risk of living, despite our fear of the exposure that living inevitably brings and the sense of tempting fate to knock us back into relapse again through aspiring to more than we deserve.

As part of trying to live with all the potential that hope opened up for her, Sedgwick wanted to move away from the detached, critical kind of reading and writing – in which she had excelled as an academic – that brought the reassuring certainties of knowledge; that, in effect, told her what she already knew; that left no space to live and think differently in the present. Instead, Sedgwick wanted to be willing to experience surprise, and that meant writing and reading differently, with an openness to uncertainty.

Not knowing in advance what we might think or feel raises the possibility of pain as well as relief, of course. It is a risk in writing, as in life, that I now think is worth taking. I don't want to keep doing things the way I used to, writing the way I used to write, feeling the way I used to feel. By refusing the self-knowledge of depression and OCD, and acting as if I do not know what might happen if I try to think, feel and act otherwise, I want to accept the traumatic experience of hope and write as if I am alive.

ᐯ

I am going home, but I am still trying to figure out the relationship between hope and home. Surely some places make it easier for us to embrace the risk of life, the future, than others? As the poet Dinah Hawken says, hope *is to do with trees*:

> being   among trees.
> It is to do with tree ferns:
> mamaku, ponga, wheki.
> Shelter under here
> is so easily
> understood.

My home on the ridge is not simply a retreat from the world; I don't want it to be that. But it *is* a shelter, a place where some things can be easily understood, if other questions necessarily remain unresolved.

Am I still trying to construct a coherent narrative of my life? Maybe; I'll leave that to you to judge. I don't ever want to be free of narratives, but I don't want to be trapped in the same old stories, even as I turn to literature again and again. The past will always be with me – it is part of what makes the present real – but it does not have to define me. I know, instead, that I need to accept the place of ambivalence about my past and the unpredictability of my future. I need more open-ended stories in my life. Such stories will inevitably be shot through with the resonances of the past, like the sheen of shot-silk that changes the way you see the fabric, showing more than you thought was there – a thousand times deeper than a present where you only deny your past, try to bury it where it can't hurt you any more. The resulting (and messy) tangle of aims, desires, fears, responsibilities, memories, questions, is what lived life is all about.

I guard my recovery jealously but I still have times when I succumb to the contamination loop, washing and sanitising my hands repeatedly until it feels okay. I touch the world more. I let it come closer. I take out the rubbish. I clean the bathroom. I use other people's pens. But if I ever met you, I wouldn't want to shake your hand.

NOTES

Epigraph

p.7   *Isn't it plain* – Mary Oliver, 'Landscape', *Dream Work*, New York: Atlantic Monthly Press, 1986, 68.

Chapter 1

p. 14   *a secretive exemption* – Adam Phillips, 'First Hates', *One Way and Another: New and selected essays*, London: Hamish Hamilton, 2013, 56.

p. 15   *In the phobic fantasy* – Phillips, 'First Hates', 56.

p. 15   *Symptoms are a way* – Phillips, 'First Hates', 18.

Chapter 2

p. 17   *To be petrified* – Phillips, 'First Hates', 56.

p. 19   *semi-mystical topography* – Elizabeth Bowen, 'The Bend Back', *The Mulberry Tree: Writings of Elizabeth Bowen*, Hermione Lee, ed., London: Vintage Classics, 1999, 55.

Chapter 3

p. 26   *Open unto the fields* – William Wordsworth, 'Composed Upon Westminster Bridge, September 3, 1802', *The Works of William Wordsworth*, Ware: Wordsworth Editions, 1994, 269.

p. 26   *Murmuring of innumerable bees* – Alfred Lord Tennyson, 'Canto VII', *The Princess*, New York: Henry Holt, 1900, 98.

p. 26   *Season of mists* – John Keats, 'To Autumn', *English Romantic Verse*, David Wright, ed., London: Penguin, 1968, 282.

p. 26   *hedge-rows, hardly hedge-rows* – Wordsworth, 'Lines Composed a Few Miles Above Tintern Abbey, On Revisiting the Banks of the Wye During a Tour, July 13, 1798', *The Works of William Wordsworth*, 206.

p. 27   *a place with more geography* – Tim Winton, *Island Home: A landscape memoir*, Clayton: Penguin Australia, 2015, 15.

Chapter 4

p. 35   *Everything is broken* – Radiohead, 'Planet Telex', track 1 on *The Bends*, Parlophone, 1995.

p. 38   *Guess that's it* – Thom Yorke, 'Default', track 9 on *Atoms for Peace*, *Amok*, XL Recordings, 2013.

p. 39   *Despair is a form* – Rebecca Solnit, 'Woolf's Darkness: Embracing the inexplicable', *Men Explain Things to Me*, London: Granta, 2014, 94.

p. 39   *The distinguishing mental features* – Sigmund Freud, 'Mourning and Melancholia', *The Standard Edition of the Complete Psychological Works of Sigmund Freud*, vol. XIV, trans. James Strachey, London: Hogarth Press, 244.

p. 40   *no [wo]man ever threw away life* – David Hume, 'Of Suicide', quoted in Simon Critchley, *Notes on Suicide*, London: Fitzcarraldo Editions, 2015, 91.

p. 40   *Only optimists commit suicide* – E.M. Cioran, quoted in Critchley, *Notes on Suicide*, 72.

p. 40   *How is one to live* – Virginia Woolf, 28 April 1897, *A Passionate Apprentice: The early journals 1897–1909*, Mitchell A. Leaska, ed., London: Pimlico, 2004 (Kindle).

p. 41   *What I want to say* – Hermione Lee, *Virginia Woolf*, London: Chatto & Windus, 1996, 756.

p. 41   *What kind of coherence* – Critchley, *Notes on Suicide*, 65, 66.

Chapter 5

p. 46   *unaliveness* – D.W. Winnicott, 'The Value of Depression', *Home is Where We Start From: Essays by a psychoanalyst*, New York: Norton, 1990, 75, 78.

p. 47   *On the ground floor* – Mark Rice-Oxley, *Underneath the Lemon Tree: A memoir of depression and recovery*, London: Abacus, 2015, 256.

p. 47   *When there is no longer* – Darian Leader, *The New Black: Mourning, melancholia and depression*, London: Penguin, 2009, 21–22.

p. 48   *There is nothing like* – Adam Phillips, 'On Success', *One Way and Another: New and selected essays*, London: Hamish Hamilton, 2013, 67.

Chapter 7

p. 53   *Closer to fine* – Emily Saliers, 'Closer is Fine', track 1 on *Indigo Girls*, Epic Records, 1989.

p. 54   *The wide glare* – Robert Graves, 'The Cool Web', *New Collected Poems*, Garden City, NY: Doubleday, 1977, 27.

Chapter 8

p. 61   *If you've ever been* – This and the following quotations from what I call *Mindfulness for Morons* are taken from a well-known mindfulness workbook which I prefer not to name.

p. 61   *hearing the grass grow* – George Eliot, *Middlemarch*, Harmondsworth: Penguin, 1980, 226.

p. 61–62 *any turn in the wheel* – Virginia Woolf, *To the Lighthouse*, Oxford: Oxford University Press, 2008, 1.

p. 62   *the quickest of us* – Eliot, *Middlemarch*, 226.

p. 62   *This spreading of some vital* – Marion Milner, *A Life of One's Own*, originally published 1934, London: Routledge, 2011, 50–51.

p. 63   *simply to press* – Milner, *A Life of One's Own*, 51.

p. 65   *Knitting is the saving* – Virginia Woolf, March 1912, *The Letters of Virginia Woolf Volume II: 1912–1922*, Nigel Nicolson and Joanne Trautman, eds, New York: Harcourt Brace Jovanovich, 1975, 491.

p. 65   *it's comforting to think* – Holly Van Houten, '"Knitting is the Saving of Life" – Virginia Woolf', *Knitted Thoughts*, 15 September 2010: www.knittedthoughts.com

p. 65   *I now feel very clear* – Virginia Woolf, March 1912, *The Letters of Virginia Woolf Volume II*, 491.

Chapter 9

p. 67 *Write as if* – Anne Lamott, *Bird by Bird: Some instructions on writing and life*, New York: Anchor Books, 1994, 99.

p. 70 *I feel that I* – Virginia Woolf, 'Sketch of the Past', *Moments of Being*, Jeanne Schulkind, ed., London: Pimlico, 2002, 86.

p. 71 *being a writer* – Lamott, *Bird by Bird*, 236.

Chapter 10

p. 75 *green-blue / green-blue* – Ursula Bethell, 'Summer Afternoon', *Collected Poems*, Vincent O'Sullivan, ed., Wellington: Victoria University Press, 1997, 46.

p. 76 *I wouldn't be a good* – Bethell, quoted in Vincent O'Sullivan's introduction, *Collected Poems*, xii.

p. 76 *Today I woke* – Bethell, 'Incident', *Collected Poems*, 13.

p. 76 *Muddy boots* – Bethell, 'Prepare', *Collected Poems*, 5.

p. 76 *I find vegetables fatiguing* – Bethell, 'Perspective', *Collected Poems*, 19.

p. 77 *a structure of excessive plainness* – Bethell, 'Detail', *Collected Poems*, 5.

p. 77 *I said: I will go* – Bethell, 'Discipline', *Collected Poems*, 9.

p. 77 *There is perpetual* – Bethell, 'Controversy', *Collected Poems*, 12.

p. 77 *the garden / is as much poem* – Jenny Bornholdt, 'Big Minty Nose', *The Rocky Shore*, Wellington: Victoria University Press, 2008, 68.

Chapter 11

p. 78 *Where do I belong?* – Richard Mabey, *Nature Cure*, London: Vintage Books, 2008, 10.

p. 82 *the sun is on the sea* – A.R.D. Fairburn, 'To a Friend in the Wilderness', *Selected Poems*, Mac Jackson, ed., Wellington: Victoria University Press, 1995, 120.

Chapter 12

p. 88 *Dogs are not surrogates* – Donna Haraway, *Companion Species Manifesto: Dogs, people and significant otherness*, Chicago: Prickly Paradigm Press, 2007, 5.

p. 92 *full-grown lambs* – Keats, 'To Autumn', *English Romantic Verse*, 282.

p. 92 *This is my last sight* – Virginia Woolf, 'Sketch of the Past', *Moments of Being*, 95.

Chapter 13

p. 93 *Those who have studied* – Edward Grey, *The Charm of Birds*, London: Weidenfeld & Nicolson, 1927, vii.

p. 94 *pine for what is not* – Percy Bysshe Shelley, 'To a Skylark', *The Major Works*, Oxford: Oxford University Press, 2003, 465.

p. 95 *bird thou never wert* – Shelley, 'To a Skylark', 463.

p. 95 *immortal Bird* – Keats, 'Ode to a Nightingale', *English Romantic Verse*, 278.

p. 95 *the achieve of* – Gerard Manley Hopkins, 'The Windhover', *Poems and Prose*, W.H. Gardner, ed., Harmondsworth: Penguin, 1963, 30.

p. 95 *the admittance of light* – Herbert Guthrie-Smith, *Tutira: The story of a New Zealand sheep station*, Edinburgh/London: William Blackwood and Sons, 1921, 207.

p. 97   *We no longer see* – Richard Smyth, 'Plashy fens: The limitations of nature writing', *Times Literary Supplement*, 8 May 2015, 14.

p. 99   *In a way, it was a relief* – Janet Frame, *Towards Another Summer*, Auckland: Random House, 2007, 15–16.

p. 99   *I was a certified lunatic* – Frame, *Towards Another Summer*, 20.

Chapter 14

p. 100 *Fitter, happier, more productive* – Radiohead, 'Fitter Happier', track 7 on *OK Computer*, Parlophone, 1997.

p. 101 *our unlived lives* – Adam Phillips, *Missing Out: In praise of the unlived life*, London: Hamish Hamilton, 2012, xvii.

p. 103 *Few other professions* – Miya Tokumitsu, 'In the Name of Love', *Jacobin*, no. 13, 2014: www.jacobinmag.com/2014/01/in-the-name-of-love/

p. 103 *This is the story* – Kate Bowles, 'Beyond a Boundary', *Music for Deckchairs*: https://musicfordeckchairs.wordpress.com/2013/12/09/beyond-a-boundary

p. 104 *a pervasive apprehension* – Andrew K. Przybylski et al., 'Motivational, emotional, and behavioral correlates of fear of missing out', *Computers in Human Behavior*, no. 29, 2013, 1841.

Chapter 15

p. 105 *Still ill* – The Smiths, 'Still Ill', track 6 on *The Smiths*, Rough Trade, 1984.

p. 106 *I read the way* – Mary Oliver, 'Staying Alive', *Upstream: Selected essays*, New York: Penguin, 2016, 16.

p. 106 *easeful Death* – John Keats, 'Ode to a Nightingale', *English Romantic Verse*, 278.

Chapter 16

p. 111 *I said no, no, no* – Amy Winehouse, 'Rehab', track 1 on *Back to Black*, Island Records, 2006.

Chapter 18

p. 126 *a mother who remains* – Andre Green, 'The Dead Mother', *On Private Madness*, London: Karnac Books, 1996, 146.

p. 127 *sinister black* – Green, 'The Dead Mother', 146.

p. 127 *a hole in the texture* – Green, 'The Dead Mother', 151.

p. 128 *becomes her own mother* – Green, 'The Dead Mother', 156.

p. 128 *This cold core burns* – Green, 'The Dead Mother', 156.

p. 129 *which remains totally hidden* – Green, 'The Dead Mother', 149.

Chapter 19

p. 131 *if the doors* – Mary Oliver, 'Landscape', *Dream Work*, New York: Atlantic Monthly Press, 1986, 68.

p. 131 *yogaphobe* – Matt Haig, *Reasons to Stay Alive*, Edinburgh: Canongate, 2015, 194.

p. 135 *the persecutor* – Adam Phillips, *Winnicott*, Cambridge: Harvard University Press, 1989, 96.

p. 136 *going-on-being* – D.W. Winnicott, 'Mind and Its Relation to Psyche-Soma', *Collected Papers:*

Through paediatrics to psychoanalysis, London: Routledge, 1958, 245.

p. 136 *play … finding through pleasure* – Phillips, *Winnicott*, 144.

p. 136 *holding environment* – D.W. Winnicott, 'The theory of the parent-infant relationship', *The International Journal of Psychoanalysis*, no. 41, 1960, 589.

Chapter 20

p. 137 *Think of the long trip* – Elizabeth Bishop, 'Questions of Travel', *Poems*, New York: Farrar, Straus and Giroux, 2011, 91.

Chapter 21

p. 145 *soaring, like birds' wings* – Virginia Woolf, *The Diary of Virginia Woolf, Volume IV: 1931–1935*, Anne Olivier Bell and Andrew McNellie, eds, Orlando: Harcourt Brace, 1982, 124.

p. 146 *the deep power of joy* – Wordsworth, 'Tintern Abbey', *The Works of William Wordsworth*, 206.

p. 150 *There is, let us confess* – Virginia Woolf, 'On Being Ill', *The Crowded Dance of Modern Life: Selected essays: Volume two*, London: Penguin, 1993, 46.

p. 150 *Directly the bed* – Woolf, 'On Being Ill', 47.

p. 151 *what one saw now* – Virginia Woolf, 'Evening over Sussex: Reflections in a Motor Car', *The Crowded Dance of Modern Life*, pp. 82–83.

Chapter 22

p. 156 *You tell yourself* – Mark Rice-Oxley, *Underneath the Lemon Tree: A memoir of depression and recovery*, London: Abacas, 2015, 256.

p. 159 *The spreading of some* – Marion Milner, *A Life of One's Own*, originally published 1934, London: Routledge, 2011, 50–51.

Chapter 23

p. 161 *bed is mother* – Helen Garner, 'White Paint and Calico', *Everywhere I Look*, Melbourne: Text Publishing, 2016, 17.

p. 164 *This is a low* – Blur, 'This is a Low', track 15 on *Parklife*, Food Records, 1994.

p. 168 *The art of losing* – Elizabeth Bishop, 'One Art', *The Complete Poems 1926–1973*, New York: Farrar, Straus and Giroux, 1983, 198.

p. 170 *What psychoanalysis, at its best* – Adam Phillips, 'The art of non-fiction no. 7', *Paris Review*, no. 208, Spring 2014: www.theparisreview.org/interviews/6286/adam-phillips-the-art-of-nonfiction-no-7-adam-phillips

p. 171 *This is what I have decided* – Elizabeth Hardwicke, *Sleepless Nights*, New York: New York Review Books, 1979, 3.

Chapter 27

p. 189 *My heart in hiding* – Hopkins, 'The Windhover', *Poems and Prose*, 30.

p. 195 *And it was my mother* – Charles Dickens, *Bleak House*, London: Penguin, 1985, 869.

Chapter 28

p. 197 *Stirred for a bird* – Hopkins, 'The Windhover', *Poems and Prose*, 30.

p. 198 *as if they're ripping books* –
Vivian Smith, 'Sulphur-Crested
Cockatoos', *Along the Line*,
Cambridge: Salt, 2006, 117.

p. 198 *sweeter than singing* – Henry
Kendall, 'Bellbirds', *Leaves from
Australian Forests*, Melbourne:
George Robertson, 1869, 45.

p. 199 *Often I sit* – Kendall, 'Bellbirds',
47.

Chapter 29

p. 202 *If you want more* – Diana Bridge,
'The route', *Porcelain*, Auckland:
Auckland University Press, 2001,
3.

p. 203 *A parent is someone* – Adam
Phillips, 'Punishing Parents', *One
Way and Another*, 352.

p. 204 *And I am aware* – Sylvia Plath,
'Tulips', *Ariel*, London: Faber and
Faber, 1965, 22.

Afterword

p. 207 *For the present* – Virginia Woolf,
'Sketch of the Past', *Moments of
Being*, 108.

p. 208 *Often a fracturing* – Eve Kosofsky
Sedgwick, 'Paranoid Reading
and Reparative Reading, Or,
You're So Paranoid, You Probably
Think This Essay is About You',
*Touching Feeling: Affect, pedagogy,
performativity*, Durham: Duke
University Press, 2003, 146.

p. 209 *Hope is to do* – Dinah Hawken,
'Hope', *Oh There You Are Tui! New
and selected poems*, Wellington:
Victoria University Press, 2001, 95.

Acknowledgements

For good or ill, I know this book would never have been written if I had not taken up a position at the University of Kent at Canterbury. Emigrating to the UK may have been a painful experience that led to the breakdown I describe in this story, but it also gave me the opportunity to work with gifted colleagues who encouraged me – by example, as well as more personally – to write in a new, more creative, way, outside the parameters of my training in scholarly research. I will always be grateful to them for that. In particular, Derek Ryan, who read the earliest draft of just a few chapters and kept reading successive drafts as they grew and changed, was a generous and meticulous reader who made sure I never gave up on this project.

There were many other Kent colleagues who provided both moral and material support when I needed it most, but I have to single out Eleri Caruana for her unstinting loyalty, good humour, and grace under pressure. Whenever I thought I had reached my lowest point during my final year in England, Eleri was always there with a smile, a shoulder to cry on and wise counsel.

My dear friend Holly Furneaux invited me to speak at an inspiring symposium entitled 'Reparative Practices: Reading, living, loving' at the University of Cardiff in 2016. This opportunity to speak publicly about my illness for the first time gave me the courage to keep writing.

I am grateful to the wonderful folk at Casa Ana in Ferreirola, Spain, where I spent two invaluable weeks trying to finish this book once and for all during a scorchingly hot Andalusian summer. Thank you to Mary-Jane Holmes (writing mentor extraordinaire), and to Gil Hodges and Jennifer Hodges Consalvi for morale-boosting conviviality. We'll always have Trevélez.

I also want to thank Rachel Scott at Otago University Press and editor Caren Wilton for all their help and advice throughout the publication process.

Finally, my whānau, the people who have been there – whatever the distance separating us – throughout the past few painful years: anything I say here would be inadequate, but thank you for putting up with me when I was such hard work.

Names other than those of my immediate family (and some place names) have been changed.